The Composition of *The Rainbow* and *Women in Love:* A History

The Composition of *The Rainbow* and *Women in Love:* A History

CHARLES L. ROSS

Published for the Bibliographical Society
of the University of Virginia by
the University Press of Virginia
Charlottesville

THE UNIVERSITY PRESS OF VIRGINIA
Copyright © 1979 by the Rector and Visitors
of the University of Virginia

First published 1979

Frontispiece: Lawrence's sketch of a visionary rainbow, sent to Viola Meynell on 2 March 1915: "I have finished my *Rainbow,* bended it and set it firm. Now off and away to find the pots of gold at its feet." (Courtesy Gerald Pollinger and the Estate of Frieda Lawrence.)

Library of Congress Cataloging in Publication Data

Ross, Charles L. 1945–
  The composition of The rainbow and Women in love.

  Includes index.
  1. Lawrence, David Herbert, 1885–1930. The rainbow.
2. Lawrence, David Herbert, 1885–1930. Women in love.
3. Lawrence, David Herbert, 1885–1930 – Criticism, Textual.
I. Virginia. University. Bibliographical Society. II. Title.
PR6023.A93R336   823'.9'12   79–1422   ISBN
0–8139–0704–7

Printed in the United States of America

To my Mother and Father

Contents

Acknowledgments	ix
Introduction	1

PART ONE

From "The Sisters" to *The Rainbow*		13
1	The Manuscripts: Three Early Versions	15
2	The Final Draft, *The Rainbow*	28
3	The Proofs: Censorship or Revision?	37
4	Vision and Revision in the Manuscripts	73

PART TWO

From "The Sisters" to *Women in Love*		95
5	The Manuscripts: Three Preliminary Drafts	97
6	The Final Draft, *Women in Love*	115
7	The Proofs: Censorship and Revision	124
8	Techniques of Revision in the Manuscripts	131

Appendix: Problems of Transmission in the Typescripts of *Women in Love*	149
Index	161

Acknowledgments

I hope this work of literary detection will have both practical and critical uses. It should aid in the restoration of D. H. Lawrence's bowdlerized texts and in the critical study of the genesis and development of his art.

It is a pleasure to acknowledge the generous assistance of individuals and institutions. My narrative benefited from the perspicacious readings of Lester Beaurline, Hans Gabler, Stephen Gill, Cecil Y. Lang, David Nordloh, and Richard Proudfoot. Mistakes of fact or emphasis are my own. The staffs of the Humanities Research Library of the University of Texas at Austin and the Thomas Fisher Rare Book Library at the University of Toronto made manuscripts available and patiently answered many questions. David Farmer, Gerald Lacy, and Keith Sagar shared their knowledge of the chronology of Lawrence's writings. Janice Cauwells helped collate the manuscripts. Laurence Pollinger Ltd. and the Estate of the late Mrs. Frieda Lawrence gave permission to quote from unpublished manuscripts. The

Acknowledgments

American Council of Learned Societies and the University of Virginia gave financial support. I am very grateful to all.

Parts of section 2 appeared in *The Library* (June 1974) and *The D.H. Lawrence Review* (Summer 1975). I thank the editors for permission to reprint these sections.

My wife, Barbara Quilligan Ross, sustained me throughout the project.

Introduction

Introduction

"*The Rainbow* and *Women in Love* are really an organic artistic whole. I cannot but think it would be well to issue them as *Women in Love*, Vol. I and Vol. II."[1] Lawrence's sweeping claim epitomizes the development of his two greatest novels from an ambitious project called "The Sisters" over the years 1913–19. They began their imaginative gestation in 1913 as an "organic artistic whole" and remained so through two laborious years of drafting until 1915, when Lawrence realized the project had become too "unwieldy" for one volume. Then *The Rainbow*, the first result of "The Sisters" project, was published in 1915. But Lawrence thought of subsequent work on *Women in Love*, finished in 1919 and published in 1920, as a continuation of "The Sisters" material: "I have finished *The Sisters* in effect. . . . It is a sequel to *The Rainbow*, but very different" (*CL*, pp. 457, 495). Consequently, one cannot understand the full

---

[1]Harry T. Moore, ed., *The Collected Letters of D. H. Lawrence* (1962; rpt. London: Heinemann, 1965), p. 615 (16 Jan. 1920). Hereafter cited in text as *CL*.

resilience of Lawrence's imagination or its exploratory daring unless one supplements criticism of the finished texts with knowledge of their growth from the one seed into an organic whole.[2]

Although it is common knowledge that the two novels developed somehow from a single source, there has been a great deal of erroneous speculation about the manner in which they did so, based on inadequate knowledge of the surviving and largely unpublished drafts. The primary concern of this study is to make a contribution to Lawrence scholarship by locating, ordering, and dating all the available materials and by analyzing their textual peculiarities.

The materials are extensive. *The Rainbow* alone cost Lawrence a prodigious amount of labor over a period of two and one-half years. He made four novel-length drafts, revising heavily along the way. The extant manuscripts and typescripts show that, in the final creative effort, Lawrence extensively

---

[2]*The Rainbow* will be cited in three editions. The first edition published by Methuen (M) will be cited when proof changes are in question. Elsewhere the current English and American editions will be used; these descend from the expurgated American edition of B. W. Huebsch. The English Penguin (P) is the best text now available because it restores the passages expurgated by Huebsch. The American Viking/Penguin (V) still retains the expurgated Huebsch text, but is the only one available to the American reading public.

Women in Love will be cited in the Modern Library edition (ML), which reprints the first edition of Thomas Seltzer (1920).

Introduction

revised the autograph manuscript, the subsequent typescript, and even the proofsheets. One of the effects of the present study should be to establish that Lawrence was often painstaking, nurturing his insights and intuitions for months and years and allowing them to grow into their inevitable shapes.

For example, the notion of a sequel is a simplification of the process by which Lawrence created and reconsidered the matter of "The Sisters." A perusal of surviving fragments of the early drafts indicates that the first draft actually contained a version of *Women in Love* and that Lawrence did not proceed to compose his "Brangwensaga" in any straightforward fashion, generation by generation. Thus the sequence of the published novel does not reflect the sequence of Lawrence's imaginative engagement with his subject.

Therefore, another effect of this study will be to show that the nature of Lawrence's creativity has been misrepresented by even his staunchest admirers, who have gone to the extreme of presenting him as something of a daimonic novelist. Praising Lawrence's creativity, for instance, Aldous Huxley wrote: "It was characteristic of him that he hardly ever corrected or patched what he had written. I have often heard him say, indeed, that he was incapable of correcting. If he was dissatisfied with what he had written, he did not, as most authors do, file, clip, insert, transpose; he rewrote. In other words, he gave the *daimon* another chance to say what it

Introduction

wanted to say."³ Huxley's description might serve for Lawrence's habits in later life, the period of Huxley's acquaintance with Lawrence and of the famous instance of *Lady Chatterley's Lover*, which exists in three virtually unrevised drafts. But it emphatically does not fit the composition of "The Sisters" project. Later F. R. Leavis, defending Lawrence against Flaubertian canons of artistry, restated Huxley's opinion with a polemical purpose:

The Rainbow and *Women in Love* . . . represent . . . an immense labour of art, an untiring solicitude to get things right. His methods of work were characteristically un-Flaubertian (and un-Joycean). It is plain from the letters and other sources that he went forward rapidly once he had started on an enterprise, writing long stretches in remarkably little time as the creative flow carried him on. The first draft written, he revised, not by correcting locally or re-working parts, but by re-writing the whole with the same kind of creative *élan* as had gone to the earlier version.⁴

The actual practice of Lawrence was far more complex and resourceful than either Huxley or Leavis implies. It was, in one critic's phrase, "exploratory"⁵

---

³Aldous Huxley, ed., *The Letters of D. H. Lawrence* (London: Heinemann, 1932, rpt. 1956), p. xvii.

⁴F. R. Leavis, *D. H. Lawrence: Novelist* (New York: Alfred A. Knopf, 1956), p. 18.

⁵Mark Kinkead-Weekes, "The Marble and the Statue: The Exploratory Imagination of D. H. Lawrence," in *Imagined*

Introduction

—firm of purpose yet sensitive to the medium of fiction and willing to leave the work fluid and adaptable, both in its parts and as a whole, for a surprisingly long period of time.

The consequences for Lawrence criticism of an understanding of his methods and manner of composition should be many and varied. By using the draft materials with the aid of a reconstructed compositional history, the critic will be able to give due weight to the many so-called sources or influences that Lawrence mentions in the letters and "pollyanalytics."[6] The critic will also be able to see the artistic practice Lawrence was attempting to describe theoretically in letters and essays and to judge the complex relation of art and didactic statement. A picture should emerge of complementary activity in different genres.

The method of following Lawrence's progress will be twofold: historical and textual. The historical context is largely supplied by his own letters, many of which have never been published. Lawrence's artistic intentions were so radical that he felt the need to explain himself to correspondents. These letters form a commentary on the novelist's artistic

---

Worlds: Essays in Honor of John Butt, ed. Ian Gregor and Maynard Mack (London: Methuen, 1968), pp. 371–418.

[6]In *Fantasia of the Unconscious* Lawrence coined "pollyanalytics" as a depreciatory title for his philosophical speculations.

Introduction

ambitions, problems, and tentative solutions. Most of our knowledge of the first two drafts of *The Rainbow*, which he burned except for two fragments, comes from letters to Edward Garnett, A. W. McLeod, Henry Savage, and others. The critic finds them a welcome companion because they reveal what Lawrence thought were the stages in his imaginative growth. At the same time, they can be misleading if used literally as guides to the fiction. The critic must compare the factual information culled from the letters with the draft materials. For example, the notorious letter to Edward Garnett of 5 June 1914 gives the impression of a sharp break with Lawrence's past practice and that of the traditional novel. Yet previous letters and surviving fragments of early drafts testify that the apparent break was actually a gradual and hesitant change. When Lawrence determined to abandon the successful novelistic vein of *Sons and Lovers*, he did not have a definite plan of action, or fictional course, plotted. In fact, his intuition largely baffled him: "I am doing a novel which I have never grasped. Damn its eyes, there I am at page 145, and I've no notion what it's about" (*CL*, p. 203). In short, Lawrence may have been prescient in predicting the bafflement of the public at a novel like *The Rainbow*, "written in another language almost" (*CL*, p. 259), but the drafts show a gradual rather than an abrupt change. The complementary textual evidence is supplied by the voluminous unpublished manuscripts.

Introduction

Although there is no space to describe in detail the content of the drafts, an attempt has been made to give some sense of the matter of the Brangwensaga in its early unpublished versions. Furthermore, a sample of the revisions in the manuscripts will indicate the use to which the scholarship can be put by critics interested in the development of the art.

It is a critical commonplace to say that Lawrence developed rapidly as a writer. In the period of "The Sisters" the development took the form of bursts of creativity, followed by reflection, and finally rewriting or wholesale revision. From the historical and textual evidence it is possible to piece together a valuable though severely limited view of growth in the early drafts of the novels. Fortunately, there is no limit to our view of the final and most significant periods of creativity. Autograph manuscripts and typescripts of the final drafts of both novels have been preserved. Lawrence made copious revisions in all, inserting autograph and typewritten sections and even revising the proofs. They afford the raw materials for a species of literary archaeology, permitting the critic to reconstruct the compositional history of "The Sisters"—that is, to follow the creative sequence of Lawrence's imagination in one of the most ambitious projects of modern literature.

First it is necessary to explain the nature and quantity of *The Rainbow* materials that are available for examination. Lawrence nearly succeeded in covering his tracks by burning "quite a thousand pages" (*CL*, p. 269), or probably the manuscripts of the initial two drafts of "The Sisters" and more. For some unknown reason two fragments consisting of fourteen autograph sheets survived the bonfire. Since Lawrence's bibliographer lists them under *Women in Love*, their identity as early fragments of "The Sisters" will have to be established.[7] A third fragment survives because Lawrence inserted it in the subsequent manuscript, apparently finding it easier to rewrite interlineally than to copy out the sixty-five-page portion of typescript in his own hand. It will be argued that this typescript fragment is all that remains of the novel's third draft. Finally, there are a complete holograph manuscript of the novel (or "original manuscript") and a typescript prepared from the holograph manuscript (or "final manuscript"), constituting the novel's fourth and final draft. For purposes of definition, the term *draft* refers to a temporal unit as well as a physical object. A draft is a version of the novel composed and revised in one continuous period of time. Thus the autograph manuscript of *The Rainbow* and the typescript subsequently prepared from it are called one draft because Lawrence worked on them continuously, beginning the revision of the typescript while sections of it were still being typed. In order to dis-

---

[7] Warren Roberts, *A Bibliography of D. H. Lawrence* (London: Hart Davis, 1963), entry E441b.

tinguish stages of composition within the draft, I shall refer to the autograph manuscript as "the original manuscript" and the typescript (including holograph insertions) as "the final manuscript."[8]

Mark Kinkead-Weekes has led the way in the analysis of the manuscripts, recovering much of the history of the three early drafts.[9] Therefore the account of the two earliest drafts will be largely a recapitulation of Kinkead-Weekes's argument. The state of knowledge regarding the final draft, however, is very different. Here his conclusions can be extended appreciably, thanks to fresh textual evidence and the discovery of many unpublished Lawrence letters. This new evidence permits both further inferences about the differences between "The Wedding Ring" and *The Rainbow* and also a far more precise reconstruction of the latter's development.[10] Moreover, a full history of *Women in Love* has never been attempted; here we shall be charting virgin land.

---

[8] Roberts, E331a and b. Compare the distinction between the penultimate and final drafts of *Women in Love*, in which case at least six months passed between the completion of the penultimate typescript and renewed work on its newly typed copy.

[9] Kinkead-Weekes, pp. 371–80.

[10] "The Wedding Ring" was the name of the third draft of *The Rainbow*, which was rejected by Methuen in the summer of 1914. See p. 22.

PART ONE

From "The Sisters" to *The Rainbow*

Chapter 1

The Manuscripts: Three Early Versions

"Sisters I"

Lawrence sent the manuscript of "the Paul Morel novel" to Edward Garnett at Duckworth publishers in November 1912 and a private foreword to the novel in January 1913. He finished the proofs of *Sons and Lovers* by early March 1913. For a time he toyed with the idea of writing a novel about the life of Robert Burns transplanted to a Derbyshire setting.[1] Soon dropping this farfetched notion, he wrote 200 pages of a novel called "The Insurrection of Miss Houghton." Revised in 1920, these formed the opening part of *The Lost Girl*. But Lawrence put aside "The Insurrection" in favor of a "pot boiler . . . which seems to have come by itself": "The pot boiler is at page 110, and has developed into an earnest and painful work—God help it and me" (*CL*, p. 197). He called it "The Sisters." Predicting it would be 300 pages long, he wrote 256 pages by early June (*CL*, p. 208) and finished by 11 June 1913. He was

---

[1] Edward Nehls reprints the fragmentary Burns novel in *D. H. Lawrence: A Composite Biography*, I (Madison: Univ. of Wisconsin Press, 1957), 184–95.

already aware that it would need to be completely rewritten, as he assured Edward Garnett, who had read and criticized the "first half" (*CL*, p. 209): "I was glad of your letter about The Sisters. Don't *schimpf*. I shall make it all right when I rewrite it. I shall put it in the third person. All along I knew what ailed the book. But it did me good to theorize myself out, and to depict Frieda's God Almightiness in all its glory. That was the first crude fermenting of the book. I'll make it into art now" (*CL*, p. 208). In the same letter Frieda agrees with Garnett's criticism of the "remarkable females": "they are *me*, these beastly, superior, arrogant females" (*CL*, p. 207). Her allusion to her habit of sweeping generalization as "Ella-ing" implies that the character through whom the "God Almightiness" was projected was named Ella. Moreover, Ella probably appeared in the first half of "The Sisters," as Lawrence had not yet sent Garnett the second half (*CL*, p. 209). Thus it seems that the first draft was written in the first person and that it contained a pair of "remarkable females," one of whom was called Ella and modeled on Frieda.

In the Texas collection of Lawrence manuscripts, grouped with the drafts of *Women in Love*, are preserved two fragments of the early drafts of "The Sisters."[2] Kinkead-Weekes has identified the first fragment, numbered pages 291-96, as belong-

---

[2] Roberts, entry E441b.

ing to this first draft, or "Sisters I." He makes the identification on two grounds. First, it is written on the same paper as that used for the foreword to *Sons and Lovers*: "unusually large folio paper of poor quality, presumably Italian."[3] This is likely because Lawrence both wrote the foreword and began "The Sisters" in Gargano, Italy, whence he moved to Irschenhausen, Germany, and the summer house of Frieda's brother-in-law (*CL*, p. 202), where he finished the draft. Secondly, as the fragment concerns the end of Gerald and Gudrun's story, it must come in the second half of the draft. Therefore the page count would agree roughly with Lawrence's prediction of 300 pages. The only difficulty is that the fragment is not written in the first person; but that can be explained by the fact that it may not have been written in the same voice as that of the first, or Ella's, half.

The fragment is a scene between Gudrun, Gerald, and Loerke. Gerald has made up his mind, after six weeks, to marry Gudrun, who is pregnant with his child. Meanwhile, humiliated and desperate, she has turned to Loerke, a German sculptor, as a possible father for the child. Loerke is with her when Gerald arrives to propose. Exposing his moral and emotional obtuseness, Gerald is stunned by Gudrun's passionate resentment at his mistreat-

---

[3] Kinkead-Weekes, p. 414 n. 31. I follow his usage in referring to the two fragments as "Sisters I" and "Sisters II."

From "The Sisters" to *The Rainbow*

ment: "Why should I marry you, when you have treated me like the cheapest thing. I don't trust you. I want to know why this sudden change" ("Sisters I," p. 292). Gerald "lamely, but doggedly," repeats his excuse: "I didn't *know*." The tension between the two suitors and the resentful woman reaches a climax after Gerald threatens the sculptor: "The sculptor was showing all his teeth, like an animal, with suffering and passion. Gerald Crich flushed, then shrank. He sat crumpled upon the chair. Somehow he felt the old shame of his murdered brother, of his miserable father, of his own falsity. He seemed choked in the mud of his shame. Suddenly he flung up his face blindly, crying stubborn with misery: 'I didn't know' " (p. 293). Loerke realizes that his suit has failed, and leaves. Gerald's cry of shame and admission moves Gudrun, although his actions have killed much of her love for him:

Something in her had shut up, or gone frozen, during that time, and was now unresponsive to him, dead to him. It made a silence fall darkly inside him. There were enough shadows over them both, to start with. But he would get it all right. . . . He knew he would be able to submit to suffering. In his new conversion, he had almost a passion for submission: it was so new a thing to him. But he would never submit to fail in getting her love. That he made up his mind to. (Page 295)

The fragment ends on this ambiguous note of resolution.

In addition to the main action, Gerald's sister Winifred and his mother make brief appearances. The mother is described as "barbaric. The womanliness, the care was missing from her. She had almost lost her touch with conventional life, but lived alone, a blind, unconscious existence. For the most part, she just lay passive. . . . she was out of place, born into the wrong age" (p. 291). She is clearly the forerunner of the weird, maddened Mrs. Crich of *Women in Love*. In fact, even from a brief sketch it is obvious that the fragment contains several of the seeds of the later novel.[4]

"Sisters II"

In June and July 1913 Lawrence and Frieda visited England. When he returned to Irschenhausen, Lawrence made two false starts during August. The autumn, however, witnessed a new burst of energy: "*The Sisters* has quite a new beginning — a new basis altogether. . . . It is much more interesting in its new form" (*CL*, p. 223). Nevertheless, his expectation "to have it done in a month" proved optimistic (*CL*, p. 224); and he did not actually finish until late January 1914, when he may have abandoned the fi-

---

[4]Indeed, Kinkead-Weekes calls it the "Ur-version of *Women in Love*" (p. 375).

nal portion in response to severe criticism from Edward Garnett.[5]

Fortunately, a fragment of the second draft survives. The second fragment in the Texas collection, grouped with the *Women in Love* material and numbered pages 372–80, appears to be part of this draft, or "Sisters II." Shortly after 30 December 1913 Lawrence sent Garnett "the first half of *The Sisters*" (*CL*, p. 259), which was approximately 200 pages long.[6] Although nothing of this half survives, Lawrence provides a few clues to its contents when defending the work against Garnett's charges: "I agree with you about the Templeman episode. In the scheme of the novel, however, I *must* have Ella get some experience before she meets her Mr. Birkin" (*CL*, p. 263). The second half was the story of Ella and Birkin: "tell me whether you think Ella would be possible, as she now stands [i.e., in 150 pages of the second half], unless she had some experience of love and of men. I think, impossible. Then she must have a love episode, a significant one. But it must not be a Templeman episode" (*CL*, p. 263). Since the extant fragment consists mainly of a scene early in Ella's relationship with Birkin, we may suspect that the Gudrun-Gerald story has been dropped altogether and that the focus of about the

---

[5] See Lawrence's letter to Garnett of 29 Jan. 1914, *CL*, p. 263.

[6] Inferred from *CL*, p. 230: "When I get to page 200 I shall send you the MS. for your opinion."

first 250 pages is Ella's episode with Templeman. Certainly in all the subsequent drafts up to *The Rainbow*, the Gudrun-Gerald story does not appear. Lawrence says nothing further about it in the letters, while he does discuss the vicissitudes of Ella's story. The explanation may be that, beginning with the second draft and continuing through the completion of *The Rainbow*, he concentrated on Ella's story and shelved that of the other couple. At the very least, the order of the couples' stories has been altered. But it is implausible that Lawrence would have attempted to include the Gerald-Gudrun story in so small a compass. Kinkead-Weekes argues plausibly that "the second *Sisters* was not a rewriting of the first, but rather an attempt to get behind it, into the past."[7] As only eleven days elapsed between Lawrence's assurance that "the second half . . . will not take me long" (*CL*, p. 263) and his beginning of the third draft (*CL*, p. 264), he could not have written much more of "Sisters II" beyond the fragment.

A précis of the fragment will indicate the development of the Ella-Birkin relationship in the later part of the draft. It opens with Ella leaving Birkin's rooms "trembling, flushed, ashamed." As yet neither has made any real commitment to the relationship. Ella leaves feeling "free of him," and Birkin damps down his "rage" because he is a "gentleman." Later he calls on Ella, who is alone at home singing sentimental songs and mulling over their relation-

[7]Kinkead-Weekes, p. 376.

ship: "She wanted to understand him: she wanted to understand man: she wanted to understand Rupert Birkin. She hunted everywhere for understanding of herself and him." At first they make conversation nervously. Then suddenly they embrace, Ella "crying, in a muffled, tortured voice: 'Do you love me?'" The embrace triggers a recurrence of her old grief at the failed affair with Ben Templeman, and she collapses, convulsed. Birkin is shaken by the simultaneous manifestations of their love and her grief. Several days later they exchange letters, foreshadowing the continuance of their relationship.

"The Wedding Ring"

Lawrence began the third draft by 9 February 1914: "I have begun my novel again—for about the seventh time. I hope you are sympathizing with me. I had nearly finished it. It was full of beautiful things, but it missed—I knew that it just missed being itself. So here I am, must sit down and write it out again" (*CL*, p. 264).[8]

In early April 1914, having written "two-thirds" of "The Wedding Ring," as he now called the novel,

---

[8] It is more likely that Lawrence was indicating his energy and dedication than being specific about the number of false starts.

he burned "quite a thousand pages" of the manuscripts of the two earlier drafts.[9] The novel was much longer than either "Sisters I" or "Sisters II," "a *magnum opus* with a vengeance" (*CL*, p. 275). Frieda suggested the title "The Rainbow" when it was almost finished. Thomas Dunlop typed several copies of the manuscript by 16 May 1914 (*CL*, p. 276). Duplicates were then submitted to Methuen in London, with whom Lawrence had signed a contract on 1 July, and to Mitchel Kennerley in New York.[10] By 10 August 1914 Lawrence knew of Methuen's refusal to publish the novel on the grounds of its indecency.[11] So much do the published letters tell.

Fortunately, a portion of "The Wedding Ring" typescript has also been preserved, as part of the holograph manuscript of *The Rainbow*. Writing out *The Rainbow*, or fourth draft of "The Sisters," Lawrence decided that it would be easier to incorporate a long section of the rejected version into the

---

[9]There is no reason to doubt that he carried out his intention, expressed in a letter to John Middleton Murry: "I have written quite a thousand pages that I shall burn" (*CL*, p. 269).

[10]See letter to Amy Lowell of 18 Sept. 1915, in S. Forster Damon, *Amy Lowell: A Chronicle* (Boston: Houghton Mifflin, 1935), p. 270.

[11]Report of Proceedings at the trial of *The Rainbow*, *London Sunday Times*, 14 Nov. 1915, cited in John Worthen, "The Critical Reception of Lawrence's Earlier Novels," Diss., Univ. of Kent, 1969.

From "The Sisters" to *The Rainbow*

holograph manuscript, rewriting interlineally. The typescript, originally numbered pages 219–75 and 279–84 and renumbered 548A–604 and 608–13, must be part of "The Wedding Ring," occupying a position in the chronology of composition between "Sisters II" and *The Rainbow*. It must have been written after "Sisters II," for two reasons. First, as Kinkead-Weekes observes, "*The Wedding Ring* is the only previous version we know to have been typed, by Dunlop, and this typescript is faint enough to be a second carbon."[12] Secondly, in the excerpt Ella recalls her relationship with "Charles" Skrebensky, who is evidently the fictional replacement for Ben Templeman. It is equally clear that the fragment must have been written before the original holograph manuscript of *The Rainbow*, for five reasons, all deduced from textual evidence. The handwritten pages preceding and following the inserted typescript are both copied and revised from the typescript, indicating that the holograph version is later. Lawrence added reference to Winifred Inger, changed "Charles" to "Anton," and wrote in "Chapter X, the Widening Circle."[13] Finally, the revised pagination is 330 pages ahead of the original.

---

[12]Kinkead-Weekes, p. 414 n. 31.

[13]Original manuscript, p. 596. "Original" and "final" distinguish the two manuscripts that make up the final draft. The "original Ms." is listed as E331a in Robert's bibliography, "final Ms." as E331b.

The Manuscripts

Kinkead-Weekes has shown that the probable contents of "The Wedding Ring" may be recovered by using the pagination and the hints in the letters as a basis for speculation. However, his argument, while correct as far as it goes, is so cryptically expressed that it calls for expansion. He reasons that, since Charles Skrebensky is mentioned in the typescript, Ella has already had an early experience of lovemaking with him. In a letter of 1 February 1915 Lawrence says he has written "450 pages out of 600 or so."[14] Page 450 of the original manuscript of *The Rainbow* corresponds to page 300 in the Penguin edition, following Ursula's handholding with Skrebensky in church and their first kiss. Also, by this date Lawrence had decided to split the novel in two (*CL*, p. 306). Kinkead-Weekes then assumes that Lawrence was composing *The Rainbow* with "The Wedding Ring" before him, and that he planned to end the novel after the final failure of Ursula's affair with Skrebensky. The deduction follows that there were 150 pages (600 less 450) of "The Wedding Ring" from the first kissing episode to the final failure with Skrebensky. If so, the 65 pages of surviving typescript came somewhere near the beginning of this 150-page stretch. But "The Wedding Ring" also included an abridged version of the Ursula-Birkin story. Another letter, sent while Lawrence was still writing "The Wedding Ring," implies that

[14]Huxley, ed., *Letters*, p. 219.

the story occupied at least 80 pages (*CL*, p. 272). Finally, a linking section between the failure with Skrebensky and the meeting with Birkin may be assumed. An approximate reckoning of the length of "The Wedding Ring" is therefore possible. By adding the 200 opening pages indicated by the pagination to the predicted sections of 150 and 80 pages, and by allowing for an additional linking section, one gets "a novel of 475–500 pages, folio typescript, depending on the length of the linking section between the two love affairs."[15] Furthermore, it is likely that Kinkead-Weekes's estimated total should be revised upwards by about 125 pages, because the paper on which "The Wedding Ring" is typed is considerably longer than the paper used for either the original manuscript or the final manuscript of *The Rainbow*.[16]

While it is interesting to know the approximate length of the draft, the most important piece of information can be culled directly from the pagination, namely, the increased space (some 200 pages)

---

[15]Kinkead-Weekes, p. 379.

[16]The sheets of the original Ms. and of the final Ms. of *The Rainbow* are almost exactly the same size (9" and 7/8" × 7" and 7/8" and 9" and 15/16" × 7" and 15/16", respectively) and have nearly the same word count. This similarity may have misled Kinkead-Weekes, who overlooks the discrepancy between the sheets of "The Wedding Ring" and those of the original Ms. "The Wedding Ring" sheets measure 13" × 8", or roughly one-fifth to one-fourth longer than the original sheets.

devoted to Ella's childhood and girlhood. Apparently the trend noticed in the development from "Sisters I" to "Sisters II" continued in "The Wedding Ring": Lawrence probed deeper into Ella's past. The probable result was a new detailed account of her parents, Will Brangwen and Anna, which gave the novel a generational depth. With "The Wedding Ring," then, Ella's story became part of a family history, a "Brangwensaga."[17]

[17]Kinkead-Weekes assumes plausibly that the draft ends with the marriage of Ella and Birkin and speculates that " 'The Wedding Ring' may have included, then, the story of Ella's parents, her childhood and youth, the first girlish affair, Brinsley Street School, the Schofields, University and the second affair with Skrebensky, a return to schoolteaching, and the final finding of themselves of Ella and Birkin" (p. 379).

CHAPTER 2

The Final Draft, *The Rainbow*

The creative distance between "The Wedding Ring" and *The Rainbow* can be gauged still more precisely. For in addition to the pagination of "The Wedding Ring" typescript and the hints in the letters (both published and unpublished), there is the textual evidence of the original manuscript and the final manuscript of *The Rainbow*. It is ironic that Methuen's impertinent refusal to publish "The Wedding Ring" gave Lawrence the opportunity to pause, reconsider, and thoroughly revise the novel. He took creative advantage of even outright rejection.

The labor over the revisions of short stories for *The Prussian Officer* in the summer of 1914 and the writing of *The Study of Thomas Hardy* that fall released new energies in Lawrence. Immediately after finishing the latter in late November he began the fourth full-scale drafting of "The Sisters": "I am working *frightfully* hard — rewriting my novel" (*CL*, p. 295). By 5 December 1914 he sent the first batch of 100 pages to J. B. Pinker (his literary agent), saying that he was writing with such concentration that

The Final Draft

he had given up typing, although he had typed some: "It is a beautiful piece of work. . . . the body of it is so new" (*CL*, p. 296). A month later he sent the second hundred pages and announced his decision "to split the book into two volumes: it was so unwieldy" (*CL*, p. 306). And by 1 February 1915 he had written "450 pages out of 600 or so."[1]

As we have seen, page 450 of the original manuscript corresponds to approximately page 200 of "The Wedding Ring" typescript. Therefore, even taking into account the longer pages of the typescript, the opening section of *The Rainbow* represents an expansion of 150 to 200 pages. In what does the difference consist? Prima facie the "new body" of the novel is the first generation of the Brangwens, Tom and Lydia. It is probable that the first generation came to Lawrence as a fresh inspiration when he began to rewrite the rejected "Wedding Ring." Chapters 1 to 3 of *The Rainbow*, 140 pages in autograph, were the bulk of the novel's new body, which forced Lawrence to abandon the idea of including Ursula's experiences with Birkin in the one volume. Hence his apparently sudden decision, after almost two years of effort, to split the unwieldy project of "The Sisters" in two.

The original manuscript confirms the impression one gets from the letters of Lawrence's excitement at bursting into new seas. Pages 1 to 7 are typed, ap-

---

[1] Huxley, ed., *Letters*, p. 219.

From "The Sisters" to *The Rainbow*

parently replacing 14 handwritten pages, but in fact adding one-third again as many words.[2] Lawrence said that he "began to type" the manuscript, but soon left off. In October 1914 Amy Lowell had made Lawrence the present of a typewriter,[3] which he had trouble mastering, as a typed letter to Kotelianksy explains: "Why does my typewriter print double, have you any idea? . . . My typewriter is a Smith's Premier, No. 2. I think it is a good one, but it distresses me much by printing double. I suppose I tap it wrong."[4] Comparing the letter to the seven typed pages, it is obvious that Lawrence typed both on Miss Lowell's machine. He greatly expanded the first fourteen pages of the manuscript as he was typing, adding almost the entire opening section of chapter 1 after he had composed roughly 100

---

[2] The pagination of the holograph Ms., which continues from the typescript without a break, begins at p. 15. Each page of the typed portion contains approximately 600 words, while each page of the Ms. has approximately 220 words. The typed portion has approximately 4,200 words, whereas the fourteen missing pages of Ms. probably had approximately 3,000. Therefore, Lawrence expanded the Ms. while typing, adding more than 1,000 words.

[3] Lawrence to Amy Lowell, 14 Oct. 1914, Harvard University Library, Cambridge, Mass.

[4] The original of this letter is in the British Library. It has been published in G. J. Zytaruk, ed., *The Quest for Rananim: D. H. Lawrence's Letters to S. S. Koteliansky* (London: McGill-Queen's Univ. Press, 1970), p. 11.

The Final Draft

pages.[5] Thus the famous opening evocation of the relationship between the Brangwens and the universe came to Lawrence after he had created a large part of the Tom-Lydia generation. In terms of inspiration, then, the opening was the last altogether unforeseen section to be created. Lawrence finally saw the overarching structure of the Brangwens moving gradually, generation by generation, into history; and he shored up the structure with a late but vital cornerstone.

As the original manuscript is 707 pages long, however, the question still remains why Lawrence mistakenly estimated a novel of "600 pages or so." In the first place, it seems likely that "The Cathedral" chapter was not in "The Wedding Ring" but was new to *The Rainbow*. This is suggested by the facts that the visit to Lincoln is not chronological, having occurred several years before the action of the previous chapter, and that the original manuscript treatment is tentative, unsuccessful, and heavily revised. Then, as Kinkead-Weekes notes, Ursula's episode with Winifred Inger must be new to *The Rainbow* because Lawrence wrote a reference to Winifred into the fragment of "The Wedding Ring" typescript preserved as part of the original manu-

---

[5]See *CL*, p. 296, where the implication is that Lawrence began to type the first 100 pages of handwritten manuscript but broke off.

script.[6] Also, in the same chapter, "Shame," a distinctive strand of vocabulary appears for the first time. Uncle Tom, manager of the Wiggiston colliery, recognizes his mate in Winifred because they share a "marshy, bitter-sweet corruption"; they are "clayey," "marshy," and "foetid" in contrast to Ursula, "who was so dry and fine in her fire." The insight fired Lawrence's imagination, and he continued the examination of the marshy, corrupt element in the character of Skrebensky, who returns from the Boer War with "the strange blood-fear," knowledge of "the hot, fecund darkness" of Africa. Having discovered this aspect of his theme more than halfway through the original manuscript, Lawrence returned in the typescript to revise and expand the final sensual encounter of Will and Anna (chapter 8), endowing it with a "sinister," "terrifying," "tropical" beauty. As well as testifying to the exploratory nature of Lawrence's art, the revisions make it likely that Wiggiston and much of the later development of Skrebensky's character were not envisaged at the time Lawrence thought the novel would be "600 pages or so."

Indeed, still more suggestive evidence exists for this hypothesis. In the same letter of 1 February 1915, in which he predicts the 600-page length, Lawrence assures Pinker that "there shall be no very flagrant love-passages in it (at least to my

---

[6]Kinkead-Weekes, p. 415 n. 42.

The Final Draft

thinking)." Kinkead-Weekes thinks "this *might* suggest that the beach scene had not yet occurred to [Lawrence]."[7] His guess is almost certainly correct — for two reasons he does not adduce.

First, in an unpublished letter to Ottoline Morrell provisionally dated 11 February 1915, Lawrence describes the Sussex Downs in a way almost identical to Ursula's vision of the downs in the novel. One should compare the following description from the letter to that in the novel:

It was so beautiful on the downs today, with the sea so bright on one hand, and the down so fresh, and the floods so blue on the other hand, away below, washing at the little villages. I don't know why, but my heart was so sad, almost to break. A little train ran through the floods, and steamed so valiant into the gap. And I seemed to feel all humanity, brave and splendid, like the train, and so blind, and so utterly unconscious of where they are going or what they are doing.[8]

In the novel Ursula weeps at the futility of the train, which "had tunnelled all the earth, blindly, uglily." She turns for solace to the downs, "that cared only for their intercourse with the everlasting skies," forcing Anton to make love to her out of doors: "She took off her clothes, and made him take off all his, and they ran over the smooth, moonless turf, a long

[7] Ibid., n. 43.
[8] Lawrence to Ottoline Morrell, Humanities Research Library, University of Texas at Austin, dated by Gerald Lacy.

way, more than a mile from where they had left their clothing, running in the dark, soft wind, utterly naked, as naked as the downs themselves. . . . She took him . . . it was as if the stars were lying with her and entering the unfathomable darkness of her womb, fathoming her at last."[9] The candor of the scene, and the fact that it initiates a series of ever more violent love contests culminating in Anton's annihilation beneath the moon, suggests a sudden expansion of treatment.

Secondly, it appears that at the time he was writing Skrebensky's return from Africa, Lawrence first hit upon the striking "metallic-corrosive" vocabulary in which he describes the love contests, or battles of will, between Ursula and Skrebensky. Page 663 of the original manuscript marks the initial appearance of this metaphoric complex: "The same iron rigidity, as if the world were made of steel, possessed her again. It was no use turning with flesh and blood to this arrangement of forged metal."[10] Armed with this newfound verbal power, Lawrence rises to the description of the couple's destructive lovemaking: "He came to her, and cleaved to her very close, like steel cleaving and clinching on to her. . . . The salt, bitter passion of the sea. . . . He felt himself fusing down to nothingness, like a bead that rapidly disappears in an incandescent flame. . . . she was like

[9] V, p. 464; P, p. 465.
[10] V, p. 443; P, p. 443.

metal, he heard her ringing, metallic voice, like the voice of a harpy to him."[11]

These explicit love scenes made Lawrence less sure of the publisher's reaction: "tell me which parts you think the publisher will decidedly object to" (*CL*, p. 328), he asked Viola Meynell, who had undertaken to type the manuscript. Yet the vocabulary opened up new possibilities for his art. Thus, in the original manuscript he revised completely the Stackyard scene, making of it a verbal tour de force based on the new dimension of vocabulary. The direction of the revision—back to the Stackyard scene after the inspiration of the novel's concluding episodes— supports the hypothesis that Lawrence's deepening knowledge and treatment of Ursula's affair with Skrebensky accounts for the expansion of the original manuscript from "600 or so" to 707 pages.

Lawrence completed the original manuscript of *The Rainbow* by 2 March 1915, writing at the bottom of the last page: "End of Volume I. Greatham. March 2nd 1915." Viola Meynell volunteered to type the manuscript, sending batches of typescript to Lawrence, who gave them the final "run through" (*CL*, p. 328). Lawrence sent these batches to Lady Ottoline, who in turn forwarded them to J. B. Pinker.[12] By now Lawrence was sure that the novel

---

[11]V, pp. 471, 477–78; P, pp. 472, 478–79.

[12]"Pinker writes to me that he wants to have my novel set up in type, to avoid futile delay again. Would you send him the

From "The Sisters" to *The Rainbow*

would be controversial: "I hope you are willing to fight for this novel," he wrote Pinker, "I'm afraid there are parts of it Methuen won't want to publish" (*CL*, p. 334). Foreseeing the need for compromise, he said he would be willing to "take out sentences and phrases" but not "paragraphs or pages." On 30 April he had revised one-half of the typescript;[13] and on 31 May he mailed the last batch to Pinker (*CL*, p. 346).

MS as soon as you can." These sentences were silently omitted by Moore in *CL*, p. 333. The letter (19 Apr. 1915) is in the Humanities Research Library.

[13]Lawrence to Pinker, in possession of W. Forster, London.

CHAPTER 3

The Proofs: Censorship or Revision?

Early in July he began correcting the proofs,[1] reaching page 192 by 26 July (*CL*, p. 357) and finishing in early August. These proof sheets do not survive, but Lawrence's revisions can be deduced by comparing the typescript with the published novel. The comparison reveals that Lawrence seized the opportunity to revise the proofs with a gusto and thoroughness reminiscent of Balzac's practice. There are more than 1,500 substantive variants and 400 accidentals, ranging in kind from minute alterations to the excision of two entire pages. Thus, *The Rainbow* is unique among Lawrence's novels in being the most heavily revised in the proof stage of composition. The histories of *Sons and Lovers*, *Women in Love*, and *Lady Chatterley's Lover* substantiate our notion of Lawrence's prolonged creative struggles, but none show significant recasting at the eleventh hour. Almost every page of *The Rainbow* bears witness to the

[1] Lawrence to Pinker, 13 July 1915, Humanities Research Library.

thoroughness of this phase in the novel's revision. For what Lawrence misleadingly called "corrections" amount to scrupulous and copious revisions. Not surprisingly, Methuen was annoyed at the pervasiveness of the corrections. A member of the firm penciled numbers next to most of the changes in chapter 1, reaching number 106 before abandoning the attempt to calculate precisely the quantity. The advance was reduced from fifty pounds to thirty-three as a sign of displeasure.[2]

If this were the complete history of the proof revisions, an editor would have no reason to doubt the authority of almost all the substantive changes made between the final manuscript and the first edition, with the exception of errors resulting from the usual hazards of transmission. In fact, however, an editor's decision in approximately fifty cases would be made much more difficult by the presence of editorial pressure amounting to censorship in the proof stage of composition. There were thus two motives, or intentions, behind the altering of the proofs. Lawrence was eager to improve his artistry and to avoid censorship and suppression. The difference is one between the judgment of the artist and that of the man.

[2] On 29 May 1915 Lawrence mentions the "50 pounds due to me" (*CL*, p. 345); on 5 Oct. he thanks Pinker for sending on "the cheque for 33 pounds from Methuen," but complains that Methuen is "rather stingy about corrections of proof" (in possession of Forster).

The Proofs

The fact that Lawrence encountered editorial pressure cannot be doubted, though its extent may be. While the proofs were being prepared and revised, Pinker, acting on instructions from Methuen, forced Lawrence to make a number of changes in the text. True to his word, he complied by changing some "phrases" but stood firm against alteration of "passages and paragraphs." On 26 July 1915 he reiterated his position: "I have cut out, as I said I would, all the *phrases* objected to. The passages and paragraphs marked I cannot alter. There is nothing offensive in them, beyond the very substance they contain. And that is no more offensive than that of all the rest of the novel. . . . And I can't cut them out, because they are living parts of an organic whole" (*CL*, p. 356). Having struggled for so long to create the natural shape of his novel, he bridled at suggestions that he mutilate it. Hence, the promise to look at the slips Pinker had sent was given reluctantly, with more zeal devoted to the reasons why he could not comply than to the ways in which he would do so. The letter also testifies to Lawrence's courage and artistic integrity, for at the time he was newly married and almost destitute.

Yet, according to Pinker's version of events, Lawrence yielded to most of Methuen's demands for bowdlerization. After the novel had been banned and burned as obscene, Pinker wrote to G. H. Thring of the Society of Authors in order to defend Lawrence against the lesser charge of intransigence:

From "The Sisters" to *The Rainbow*

I gather it was suggested that Mr. Lawrence had been unyielding on the question of alterations. This is not the case. When the MS. [of "The Wedding Ring"] was delivered the publishers told me that their reader reported it as impossible for publication in its existing form. I told Mr. Lawrence of the criticism, and asked him to reconsider the MS. and Mr. Lawrence not only reconsidered it but decided that he would rewrite the novel. This he did, and the new version [*The Rainbow*] was then delivered to Messrs. Methuen. They considered it still too frank in places, and I asked them to indicate the particular passages, in order that I might ask Mr. Lawrence to modify them. This Mr. Lawrence did. He only left unchanged, I think, one passage of which they had complained.[3]

The degree to which Lawrence yielded is a vexed question. Did he make only slight changes, as he said, or almost every change demanded by Methuen, as Pinker asserted? The answer will be of crucial importance to the editor concerned to restore

---

[3]Letter of 16 Nov. 1915, *TLS*, 27 Feb. 1969. The story of the suppression of *The Rainbow* by the police and courts has been amplified recently by John Carter and other correspondents in the pages of the *TLS*, especially 27 Feb. and 17 Apr. 1969. The novel was published on 30 Sept. 1915 in an issue of 2,500 copies. On 3 Nov. a detective inspector Draper visited Methuen with a court order empowering him to seize all copies on the premises. Methuen surrendered without a fight and distributed the type on 5 Nov. without informing either Lawrence or Pinker of their action. Detective Draper returned on 11 Nov. to seize all remaining copies and to inform the publisher that he was called upon by the court to show cause why "the said

The Proofs

Lawrence's final intentions insofar as they can be reconstructed. In the absence of letters from Pinker to Lawrence, all that can be said with absolute certainty is that more than fifty substantive variants in the Methuen first edition that are not present in the final (or printer's copy) manuscript seem suspiciously uncharacteristic of Lawrence's thematic concerns and linguistic habits as they can be studied in the unpublished manuscripts.

How, then, might the future editor of the novel proceed? He will have to take risks, of course, but he need not be capricious if he is familiar with the history of Lawrence's revisions. An editor may start from the reasonable premise that the passages found objectionable by the publisher treated sexual passion or religion or both, since for Lawrence those two primary facts of human existence were inextricably connected. Then he may proceed with a few

---

books should not be destroyed." The *Guardian* reported the figure 1,011 as the number of copies condemned by the court; David Farmer estimates that some 1,002 bound copies survived because they had been sold. Lawrence's retrospective account of the court room drama is amusing: "Methuen . . . almost wept before the magistrate, when he was summoned for bringing out a piece of indecent literature. He said he did not know the dirty thing he had been handling, he had not read the work, his reader had misadvised him—and Peccavi! Peccavi! wept the now be-knighted gentleman" (D. H. Lawrence, *Phoenix*, ed. E. D. McDonald [London: Heinemann, 1936], p. 234).

From "The Sisters" to *The Rainbow*

pragmatic principles of emendation. First, if a trend of revision toward greater explicitness in the manuscripts is abruptly reversed in proof, the fact should raise suspicions of editorial pressure. As a corollary to this principle, the muting or excision of characteristic words and locutions might be suspect. A number of such interrelated or cumulative changes in a passage may be interpreted as increasing the likelihood of censorship. Although these principles in themselves cannot assure certainty, they may assist an editor in checking his intuitions. In the end there can be no theoretical or mechanical substitute for both painstaking familiarity with Lawrence's habits of composition and imaginative sympathy with his aims.

Let us turn now to a sample of the different kinds of changes that should be suspect. Cumulative changes in a scene treating human passion will raise suspicions at once. Early in the novel, before the young Tom Brangwen meets Lydia Lensky, he has several brief affairs that leave him unsatisfied, disillusioned, and liable to bouts of drinking. One is a flirtation with the mistress of a foreign gentleman whom he meets on a jaunt to Matlock, "a famous beauty spot." The version of the scene in the final manuscript describes the motivation of the young lady who, abandoned for the day by her older escort, recklessly provokes Tom to the amorous adventure. The latter half of the paragraph (enclosed in brackets) was excised from the proofs: "She was a handsome girl with a bosom, and dark hair, and blue eyes, a girl full of easy laughter, flushed from the sun, inclined to wipe her laughing face in a very natural and taking manner. [She was direct and forceful in her nature. It was dissatisfaction and anger that had led her to her form of life. Yet she had always seemed jolly.]"[4] The original version makes it perhaps too plain that Tom has succeeded in seducing her. The proof excision is given in square brackets, the replacement in angle brackets: "His heart thumped and he thought it the most glorious adventure, and was [madly in love with the girl. By gad, she was a tanger. He admired her to extremity, he almost loved her. But he did admire her, and it *was* a success.] <mad with desire for the girl.>"[5]

Finally, the most dubious change in the scene obscures both her glorying in "hard, brutal freedom" and Tom's reasons for remaining at the Inn: "She gave him an intimate smile, which made him feel [that what was between himself and her was

[4] Final Ms., p. 25; M, p. 15; V, p. 16; P, p. 22.
[5] Final Ms., p. 28; M, p. 17; V, p. 18; P, p. 23.

Square brackets surround the material that Lawrence crossed out, and angle brackets surround the revisions. This homemade system seems clear enough for the limited context of my critical examples. For a system that aims at more universal applicability, see Fredson Bowers, "Transcription of Manuscripts: The Record of Variants," *Studies in Bibliography*, 29 (1976), 212–64.

From "The Sisters" to *The Rainbow*

the right sort of thing, and what was between the other man and her was not the right sort of thing. So he wanted her to come with him. But she was too fair, and she wanted her hard, brutal freedom. She would be no man's woman. She wanted her price only. He was dark with anger.] <confused and gratified.>"[6] That she should take fierce pride in her freedom is not only plausible but of a piece with the previous mention of her "dissatisfaction and anger." The cut passage also rings true for Tom, who as an unworldly and morally conventional lad idealizes women and so wants chivalrously to defend his "light-o'-love." Any of the three cuts judged in isolation seem to be a marginal case; taken together, they excite strong suspicions that the text was muted.

The narrative of the second generation of Lawrence's "Brangwensaga" also contains changes probably made under pressure. When Anna finds herself with child (chapter 6) and wants to await her term in "innocence and bliss," she feels that her husband, jealous of her maternal self-sufficiency, is "trying to force his will upon her." In reaction she remembers the proud independence of David in the Old Testament, who uncovered himself and danced before the Lord despite the mockery of his wife Michal. In the manuscript version she recalls the biblical story and *then* decides to disrobe and dance in imitation of it. But this allusion (in brackets) has been cut in the

[6]Final Ms., p. 28; M, p. 17; V, p. 18; P, p. 24.

The Proofs

published novel, thereby disrupting the psychologically plausible transition: "She had her moments of exaltation still, re-births of old exaltations. As she sat by her bedroom window, watching the steady rain, her spirit was somewhere far off [, with David. She had always loved David. It had haunted her, how he danced naked before the Ark, and the wife had taunted him. And David had said 'It was before the Lord: the Lord hath chosen me, therefore will I play before him']".[7]

One may suspect that the reason for the excision was the reference to Anna's "love" for David and the impropriety of comparing her dance while naked with that of David "naked before the Ark." The suspicion grows when we observe that another reference to the Lord as Anna's "unseen lover" was changed to "unseen Creator," that she "loved" the story of David was diluted to read "liked," and that "shamelessly" as the adverb describing David's emotion when disrobing was altered to "exultingly." The first change is the most striking: "she danced there in the bedroom by herself, lifting her hands and her body to the [Lord, to the unseen Lover whose name was unutterable] <Unseen, to the unseen Creator who had chosen her, to Whom she belonged>".[8]

Thus the cumulative changes lead one to a near conviction that Lawrence tampered with the proofs under compulsion. Certainly the dance comes in the

[7]Final Ms., p. 280; M, p. 168; V, p. 179; P, p. 183.
[8]Final Ms., p. 280; M, pp. 168–69; V, p. 179; P, p. 183.

From "The Sisters" to *The Rainbow*

published text more abruptly and less fittingly than it had in the manuscript. Finally, as corroboration for one's choice of the manuscript reading, one might note the outrage of the public and court at precisely this passage[9] — a fair indication that the publisher's reader would have been aware of the shocking or blasphemous appearance of the scene in the eyes of the Edwardian reading public.

The next example from the second generation is both more extensive and much more problematic. It represents the case of a section which Lawrence was apparently forced to mute but which he also took the opportunity to improve while he was carrying out the dispiriting task of self-censorship. That is, one finds some changes of obviously inferior quality and others that are a distinct improvement. Moreover, there seems to be a progression whereby Lawrence began to revise from motives of compliance but finished by making truly aesthetic alterations. The section in question occupies the last half of chapter 8 ("The Child") and comprises two related scenes — Will's flirtation with Jennie the warehouse lass and his later sensual revels with Anna, which transform their marriage. The language of the scenes is deliberately "immoral and against mankind" because Lawrence believed that only by in-

---

[9]"The scene to which exception was *particularly* taken was the one where Anna dances naked, when she is with child" (*Letters from D. H. Lawrence to Martin Secker, 1911–1930*, ed. Martin Secker [Privately Published, 1970], p. 21).

dulging their repressed, shameful desires could the couple break through stalemate and find fulfillment in their private and public lives.[10] Lawrence had greatly expanded the section in revising the final manuscript, taking care to show the increasing boldness of Will, who until now has been the weak and passive partner. Indeed, the entire scene describing Will's outing to the music hall was inserted to prepare for the "blossoming out into his real self" when he returns home. Will pursues the girl with a calculation worthy of a Don Juan of the Midlands; he is quite unaware of her as a person. It would appear that Methuen, offended by the callous, predatory quality of Will's amorousness, demanded that Lawrence tone down the treatment. The effect of most of the changes in the first scene is to blunt the immediacy of Will's sensuality by substituting less concrete, more abstract language. Thus his appraisal of the "real beauties" he will relish underwent a process of euphemism:

He could see [real beauties] <distinct attractions> in her; her eyebrows, with their particular curve, gave him [profound sensual] <keen aesthetic> pleasure. Later on he would see her bright, pellucid eyes, like shallow water, and [enjoy] <know> those. And there remained the opened, exposed mouth, red and vulnerable. [Out of that

---

[10]For a discussion of the growth of the second generation from autograph manuscript through first edition, see Charles L. Ross, "The Revisions of the Second Generation in *The Rainbow*," *Review of English Studies*, 27 (1976), 277–95.

From "The Sisters" to *The Rainbow*

he would get his chief pleasure] < That he reserved as yet > .... About the girl herself, who or what she was, he cared nothing, he was quite [callous. But the features in which he felt an impersonal beauty he relished thoroughly. He wanted to come closer] < unaware that she was anybody. She was just the sensual object of his attention > ".[11]

Phrases like the last maintain a semblance of meaning while removing any emotional force. Nor do diminutions of exorbitant emotion seem consistent with Lawrence's intention to describe excessive, because frustrated, sensuality: "he only wanted to [know the touch of her] < discover her >. And [my God] through her clothing, what absolute beauty he touched [and revelled in]".[12] The effects on the girl of Will's insidious kiss were also muted in similarly uncharacteristic fashion. Of the following two changes, the first might be taken as an instance of pruning, but the second must be seen as a loss:

she too was almost swooning in the absolute of sensual knowledge. [Only as if mechanically she kept her knees closely shut together. And however absolutely she gave herself to his touch and discovery, she kept her knees tight shut, as if this were the reflex movement] ....

"Don't — don't!"

It was a rather horrible cry that seemed to come out of her. . . . There was something vibrating and beside her-

[11] Final Ms., p. 346; M, p. 213; V, p. 226; P, p. 229.
[12] Final Ms., p. 346; M, p. 214; V, p. 228; P, p. 230.

The Proofs

self in the noise. [It reminded him of the sudden terrified shriek of a rabbit in the night, when a weasel has got it.] His nerves ripped like silk.[13]

In the second scene, however, the balance seems to tip toward changes made willingly, as though Lawrence had reexamined and finally articulated the vision he had been seeking in so many drafts. We should applaud such grace under pressure and strive to separate the artistically deliberate from the adventitious. There will be marginal cases over which sensitive readers will differ, but it is surely possible to group the variants on a scale from "unlikely" (to be Lawrence's voluntary change) to "likely." The editor, in any case, cannot abdicate responsibility by merely accepting all the variants because Lawrence himself made them. Our knowledge of mixed motivation commits us to the challenge of weeding out the few compulsory changes. On the side of "unlikely" I should put a few instances of uncharacteristic wariness or awkwardness. Thus, the sentence in which Anna feels "absolved . . . from his 'goodness,' from his connection with the ten commandments of our ordered life" might have been thought sacrilegious.[14] Then too Lawrence might have been asked to excise the bloodthirsty elaboration of the cat metaphor: "He wished he were a cat, to lick her with a rough, grating lascivious tongue [, a tiger-cat

---

[13]Final Ms., p. 347; M, p. 215; V, p. 228; P, p. 231.
[14]Final Ms., p. 350.

From "The Sisters" to *The Rainbow*

to lick till the blood came, so he could lap it up till it ran from the corners of his mouth: so he could tear her flesh with his mouth]".[15] Later this passage was also cut from the American edition.[16]

But these accommodations, if such they were, are minor matters in comparison to the great number of changes that must be ranged on the side of "likely" ones. Lawrence altered several instances of flippancy in the treatment of the moral transformation of Will and Anna. Where she had said "Goodbye moral responsibilities," she came to reflect that "She adhered as little as he to the moral world."[17] And where Lawrence's archness had struck the wrong note, he provided sober summary of the moral phenomenon: "[Down went the moral fortress, the good knight was a free lance flying the banner of his own sensual desires, the good maiden was out in the wilderness enjoying herself.] <They abandoned in one motion the moral position, each was seeking gratification pure and simple.>"[18] Even more likely to represent Lawrence's second thoughts is a group of changes that continue the trend of revision in the manuscripts toward an explicit treatment of the "death" and "shame" involved in the new sensuality. In the revision of the final manuscript Lawrence had stressed that the exorbitant and even sin-

[15]Final Ms., p. 352; M, p. 220; omitted in V; P, p. 236.
[16]See p. 52 and n. 23, for the history of this edition.
[17]Final Ms., p. 350; M, p. 219; V, p. 232; P, p. 235.
[18]Final Ms., p. 351; M, p. 219; V, p. 232; P, p. 235.

ister sexual revels through which Will and Anna experience "Absolute Beauty" are a passion of death. He revised the proofs to accentuate this impression: "they lived in the [extravagances] <darkness and death> of their own sensual activities. . . . It was . . . maddening intoxication of the [flesh] <senses, a passion of death>."[19] At the same time he removed any doubts that Will and Anna are unaware of the shameful nature of their desires—a shame that must be acknowledged and somehow incorporated if they are to move beyond the old modus vivendi of reticence, frustration, and unfulfillment: "They [blotted out] <accepted> shame, and were [free of it, even in] <one with it in> their most unlicensed pleasures. [The shame simply did not exist] <It was incorporated>."[20]

Yet Lawrence insisted that the very deathliness of their sex life liberates Will, as though he feared we might overlook the positive achievement of the new sensuality in Will's released and outgoing energies. His fears have proved just; most critics follow H. M. Daleski in judging Will's involvement in woodworking classes to be "a meagre achievement."[21] That Lawrence thought otherwise can be seen in the proof revisions, where he removed any lingering traces of disparagement: "His intimate life

---

[19]Final Ms., pp. 352–53; M, pp. 220–21; V, p. 234; P, p. 237.
[20]Final Ms., p. 353; M, p. 221; V, p. 235; P, p. 238.
[21]H. M. Daleski, *The Forked Flame* (Evanston: Northwestern Univ. Press, 1965), p. 106.

From "The Sisters" to *The Rainbow*

was so [profoundly] <violently> active, that it [left a superficial man in him disengaged] <set another man in him free>. And this [superficial] <new> man turned with interest to public life, to see what part he could take in it."[22] All in all, we must wonder at the mixture of mettle and unworldliness that enabled Lawrence to make an artistic virtue of this publishing necessity.

The third generation, being the history of an emancipated woman, would have been an obvious source of concern for a prudish or timid publisher's reader. Subsequently, B. W. Huebsch, Lawrence's American publisher who had published Joyce and fought many censorship cases, felt constrained to cut six passages so that the novel would escape the fate of the English first edition.[23] Four of the six cuts

---

[22]Final Ms., pp. 353-54; M, p. 221; V, p. 235; P, p. 238.

[23]Rights for the publication of an American edition were bought by B. W. Huebsch after another American publisher, Doran, had requested alterations Lawrence was not prepared to make: "It seems The Rainbow is going to struggle out of obscurity after all—one gleam of sunshine is enough to show a rainbow" (Lawrence to Pinker, 4 Dec. 1915, in possession of George Lazarus, Slough, England). Huebsch made several expurgations without Lawrence's knowledge and then distributed the novel sub rosa so as to avoid rousing "our self-appointed censors (smut hounds as H. L. Mencken calls them) [who] would love to make a 'case' out of this" (Huebsch to Lawrence, 17 Sept. 1919, Library of Congress). The cuts, discovered when a copy of the Huebsch edition arrived in mid-Dec. 1915, made Lawrence "sad and angry" (*CL*, p. 400). Years later he read the terms of the original contract, which forbade Huebsch to

The Proofs

were made in Ursula's section. That fact alone suggests the likelihood of prepublication censorship in the preparation of the Methuen volume.

---

abridge the text without Lawrence's approval, and asked Pinker: "Did Huebsch have your permission to cut out certain parts of *The Rainbow*? He never had mine" (Lawrence to Pinker, 25 Jan. 1921, Lockwood Memorial Library, State University of New York at Buffalo).

Two hypotheses may be advanced to account for Huebsch's actions. It might have been that Pinker advised Huebsch of the passages in the novel which had been singled out as obscene by the court and that Huebsch cut those. On the other hand Huebsch may have acted on his own initiative, with the assistance of a lawyer. This version of events is favored by Marshall A. Best of the Viking Press, who worked with Huebsch from the mid-twenties until the latter's death:

"As to the specific cuts, it is clear from the published correspondence that Lawrence did not make them himself, or even see proof of them. If my considered speculation is worth anything, Huebsch made them himself — probably in consultation with his lawyer, like himself deeply involved later in the Civil Liberties Union and dedicated opponent of all censorship. They clearly agreed on the minimum they had to cut to get the book past the courts. Normal procedure in such cases, then and now, has been for the publisher to get his lawyer's opinion and then bring in the author in person or by mail. In that time of war and difficult communications, this latter step was apparently omitted" (Best to author, 5 Sept. 1975).

Fortunately, an editor need not decide which hypothesis is true or more likely, since there is no evidence that Lawrence approved the expurgations and much that he did not. Therefore, neither the Huebsch edition nor the editions of Seltzer, Secker, and Heinemann which derive from it has any textual authority.

From "The Sisters" to *The Rainbow*

In the brief interlude between the horror of teaching at Brinsley School and the commencement of college studies, Ursula is attracted to the "faun"-like Anthony Schofield, brother of fellow schoolmistress Maggie. While revising the final manuscript, Lawrence had strengthened the sexual attractiveness of Anthony, giving him the "pale grey eyes of a goat" and a "neighing laugh." It seems odd therefore that Lawrence would have voluntarily abridged Ursula's feeling of desire for Anthony. But we find a change like the following: "Her heart flamed with [desire for] <sensation of> him [for] <of> the fascinating thing he offered her."[24] Here "sensation" doesn't seem the right word for the instinctive, yearning sexuality meant by the context. Moreover, "sensation" is used directly above in a different sense, as an outwardly induced response.[25] This particular change becomes more suspicious in the light of a distinctly inferior, because vague, substitution also designed to diminish Ursula's passion for Anthony: "[She did love Anthony, though. All her life the thought of Anthony stirred in her a strong, restive passion, made her feel strong.] <She liked Anthony, though. All her life, at intervals, she returned to the thought of him and of that which he

---

[24]Final Ms., p. 623; M, p. 389; V, p. 416; P, p. 416.

[25]"Shadows and dancing moonlight were real, and all cold, inhuman, gleaming sensations" (Final Ms., p. 623; M, p. 389; V, p. 416; P, p. 416).

The Proofs

offered. > "²⁶ The pattern of changes should make an editor at least pause.

The section devoted to Ursula's affair with Anton Skrebensky contains many examples that seem even less likely to represent Lawrence's unconstrained second thoughts. In one passage as written in the final manuscript, Ursula puts her arms around Anton's "loins." The reference to the specific part of the man's body, so characteristically Lawrencean, was omitted from the first edition: "She put her arms round him, [round his loins,] and snuffed his warm, softened skin."²⁷ Nothing in the context makes the omission a plausible artistic change; it merely obscures the point that Ursula is paying innocent and spontaneous homage to Anton's physique. Moreover, the omission is of a piece with several other instances in which Lawrence removed mention of specific portions of the anatomy, like the belly and thighs, where the context makes them appropriate if not necessary. In the manuscript Will, having been denied his wife's bed, "could not bear the empty space against his breast and belly, where she used to be." The published novel drops "and belly."²⁸ When Ursula desires a "consummation" with the moon, the manuscript version has her "dashing the moonlight with her breasts and her

---

²⁶Final Ms., p. 624; M, p. 390; V, p. 417; P, p. 417.
²⁷Final Ms., p. 680; M, p. 425; omitted in V; P, p. 455.
²⁸Final Ms., p. 289; M, p. 174; V, p. 185; P, p. 188.

knees and her belly and her thighs," but the published novel retains only the references to breasts and knees.[29] Here one may think the prose ought to be hypnotic and unrestrained. And, finally, "soul" replaces the visually precise "arms," thereby disrupting the parallelism with "breast" and ignoring the context of meaning: "Skrebensky, whom she knew, whom she was fond of, who was [lovable] < attractive >, but whose [arms] < soul > could not contain her in [their] < its > waves of strength, nor his breast compel her in burning, salty passion."[30] Surely the effect of the many small changes in proof is to lessen the sensual immediacy of Ursula's experiences, as when her longing for "supreme voluptuousness" became a longing for "supreme fulfilment."[31] And surely we are compelled to question the plausibility of Lawrence's tampering in this way with a text that had grown more outspoken with each drafting.

Taken singly, the differences between the readings in the final manuscript and the published novel seem slight enough, but cumulatively they amount to a pervasive muting of the text. Fortunately, Lawrence's efforts at self-censorship were halfhearted and incomplete. As a result their incongruity in context can be noticed by the sensitive reader, even

[29] Final Ms., p. 471; M, p. 297; V, p. 317; P, p. 319.
[30] Final Ms., p. 715; M, p. 447; V, p. 477; P, p. 478.
[31] Final Ms., p. 713; M, p. 446; omitted in V; P, p. 477.

The Proofs

when they are sprinkled through the text. Therefore, there are compelling reasons to prefer the manuscript readings, which were undoubtedly the work of Lawrence the artist, to those of the first edition, which are at best conjecturally voluntary, in such cases of highly dubious change.

It may be a relief to end our examination on a humorous note. Whatever the extent of editorial interference, we may thank the obtuseness of the publisher's readers that more pressure was not applied. As Methuen explained remorsefully to the judge at the obscenity trial, his readers missed the suggestion of a lesbian relationship between Ursula and Winifred Inger:

Methuen's Lawyer: "It was . . . a remarkable thing that two members of the firm had read a certain chapter to which particular exception had been taken without conceiving the suggestion which it contained."

Sir John Dickerson, from the bench: "They cannot have read it very intelligently. It is headed 'Shame'."[32]

Although Methuen had not exacted proof changes, Huebsch cut a few lines describing the naked embrace of Ursula and her schoolmistress, to be on the safe side. We cannot wonder that henceforth Lawrence submitted to the process of publication "as to a necessary evil."[33]

---

[32]Cited in Worthen, p. 281.

[33]D. H. Lawrence, "Preface to *A Bibliography of D. H. Lawrence* by Edward D. McDonald," in *Phoenix*, p. 234.

From "The Sisters" to *The Rainbow*

Suggestions for a Critical Edition

There is a clear need to prepare a critical edition of *The Rainbow* that will constitute Lawrence's final intentions. As the discussion of editorial pressure has shown, however, the notion of "final" intentions must be clarified. It cannot mean simply the last revisions made by an author regardless of his motives. With *The Rainbow* an editor must reckon with the fact that Lawrence was forced to alter passages against his better aesthetic judgment. Such alterations may be comparatively few in number, but they affect appreciably the reader's experience of scenes in which Lawrence challenged conventional ideas of human passion and sexuality. The euphemisms should be removed in an edition dedicated to the recovery of Lawrence's final aesthetic intentions.

The resulting text should be eclectic, combining the inscriptional features of the manuscripts (accidentals) with subsequent revisions of meaning (substantives). It should admit only those substantive changes that Lawrence made willingly with an eye to artistic improvement, while rejecting those done in reluctant compliance with unsympathetic editorial demands. Such a text should also prefer the idiosyncratic flavor and meaning of Lawrence's syntax to the house styling of the publisher.

The copy text for a critical edition should be the final manuscript. The reasons for preferring the

The Proofs

final manuscript to the first edition as authority for accidentals are both practical and aesthetic. A first collation of the two states revealed more than 400 accidental variants, introduced in the galley proofs, or page proofs, or final printing. Knowing Lawrence's habits, one must doubt his attention to the correction of accidentals on their own as distinct from those connected with a substantive change. Moreover, in the cases of such isolated accidental changes, it would be impossible to judge whether Lawrence himself made or condoned the change or whether it was the result of house styling or compositorial error.[34] Finally, an aesthetic as well as a practical consideration should govern the preservation of the accidentals in the manuscript. The style of the novel deliberately attempts to mime the subject matter, conveying the rhythms of the psychic life that precedes and determines the recognizably "human" life of the characters. Lawrence strove to give not only the emotions that arise but the way in which they do so, and he defended his practice in

---

[34] Fredson Bowers has stated the rule of thumb: "The matter comes down to the point that whereas a critic can on literary grounds (aided by whatever bibliographical evidence is available) make some attempt to judge whether substantive alterations are authorial or not, no one can thus adjudicate the authority of most of the accidentals altered from the Ms. in the print" (Nathaniel Hawthorne, *The House of the Seven Gables*, ed. Fredson Bowers [Columbus: Ohio State Univ. Press, 1963], p. xlvi).

the forward to *Women in Love*: "In point of style, fault is often found with the continual, slightly modified repetition. The only answer is that it is natural to the author; and that every natural crisis in emotion or passion or understanding comes from this pulsing, frictional to-and-fro which works up to culmination."[35] This stylistic idiosyncrasy extends to the syntax of his sentences with their short, overlapping clauses punctuated by commas rather than the more conventional semicolons and periods. Any attempt to substitute normalized punctuation must be resisted in order to preserve a part of Lawrence's special distinction in the craft of fiction.[36]

The proper choice as copy text, then, would be the final manuscript. Although the earlier manuscript survives from which the final manuscript was prepared, it would not be a practicable choice. Such a modification of Greg's classic rule was foreseen by Fredson Bowers, who has identified instances of transmission in more modern books where "the substantive revision is so thoroughgoing as to generate with it a new set of accidentals."[37] This is precisely the case with the heavily revised final manuscript of

---

[35] D. H. Lawrence, *Women in Love* (New York: Modern Library, n.d.), p. x.

[36] An amusing footnote to the business of Lawrence's "incorrect" punctuation is provided by the waggish remark of the *New Statesman* reviewer: "I believe [the novel] has been accused of impropriety, but to me the most improper thing about it is its punctuation" (Worthen, p. 144).

[37] Fredson Bowers, "Multiple Authority: New Problems and

The Proofs

The Rainbow. Lawrence went over it as a whole, making substantive revisions on almost every page and revising some stretches so thoroughly that he had to insert extra holograph pages. As a result he created what constitutes, theoretically and practically, a *new* text. Therefore the final manuscript should be preferred to the earlier manuscript as copy text for a critical edition.

Thus, the editor must supplement analytical bibliography with interpretation, as E. D. Hirsch has argued: "Textual choices frequently depend upon interpretations. . . . The aim of the textual editor is to determine what the author wrote or intended to write, and no purely mechanical system which ignores interpretation could ever reliably reach such a determination."[38] The restoration of Lawrence's final intentions will require knowledge, imagination, and pluck in the art of editing.

Proof Revisions: The Virtue of Necessity

Nevertheless, the fact of editorial pressure should not be allowed to obscure the active and voluntary role Lawrence took in the proof revisions. In fact,

---

Concepts of Copy-Text," *Essays in Bibliography, Text, and Editing* (Charlottesville: Univ. Press of Virginia, 1975), p. 462.

[38]E. D. Hirsch, Jr., *Validity in Interpretation* (New Haven: Yale Univ. Press, 1967), pp. 171–72.

From "The Sisters" to *The Rainbow*

editorial pressure accounted for a very small number of alterations. The pervasive revising was largely voluntary, a final stage of creativity. A thorough enumeration and discussion of these revisions would fill a small book. What follows is a sample of the kinds of revisions showing the care Lawrence lavished on all aspects of the novel. For he was not engrossed, as were most of the reviewers, with the descriptions of physical passion.[39]

In writing and rewriting the first generation of the Brangwens, Lawrence emphasized the fact that Tom and Lydia represent the "Unknown" to each other, the entrance into a larger and more universal world that contains and validates the natural and social world of the Marsh farm. Love and the establishing of a relationship are consequently both joyous and fearful, exalting and humbling. At several places in the proofs Lawrence altered the description of Tom's awareness of the universal world in order to ennoble his character:

[He must admit that without addition he was only fragmentary, something incomplete and useless. There were all the stars in the dark heaven wandering outside him, other than himself, the whole host passing him by and ignoring him. So he sat small and poor and helpless, like a forgotten, impotent beggar as the procession goes by.]

---

[39]See, e.g., the reviews of James Douglas and Clement Shorter, reprinted in *D. H. Lawrence: The Critical Heritage*, ed. R. P. Draper (London: Routledge and Kegan Paul, 1970), pp. 93–97.

The Proofs

<He must admit that he was only fragmentary, something incomplete and subject. There were the stars in the dark heaven travelling, the whole host passing by on some eternal voyage. So he sat small and submissive to the greater ordering.>[40]

As a result of revision, Tom feels "small and submissive" but no longer an "impotent beggar"; his awareness is chastening rather than humiliating. Similarly, Lawrence heightened the consolation provided Tom by the "eternal, unchanging" world when he must endure separation from Lydia, who is suffering the birth of a child. With the discarding of the monotonous prospect of "never nearing the end," the altered paragraph closes the chapter on a more celebratory note: "The swift, unseen threshing of the night upon him silenced him and he was overcome. He turned away indoors, humbly. [The hands of joy were thrusting forward her pain, and he must not believe only in the horror. He sat by the fire enduring the slow procreation of pain, footstep after footstep, moment after moment, stride after stride, and never nearing the end.] <There was the infinite world, eternal, unchanging, as well as the world of life.>"[41]

In chapters 4 and 5, Lawrence added delicate touches to the portrait of Tom, who is trying to come to terms with the approaching marriage of his

---

[40] Final Ms., p. 57; M, p. 32; V, p. 35; P, p. 40.
[41] Final Ms., p. 122; M, p. 71; V, p. 76; P, p. 81.

daughter. Lawrence movingly renders the conflicting emotions of an aging father who finds satisfaction in the memory of his wedded life but who still rages at the old age which inevitably separates him from the life of his daughter. In cumulative strokes Lydia becomes "poignant" and "his fulfilment," rather than merely "beautiful" and "the unknown"; and their marriage "eternal" rather than "sufficient."[42] Tom curses himself for his unwillingness to "yield place," which makes him appear "like a large demon" blocking the path of life.[43] Lawrence increased the exacerbation: "he had known satisfaction with his wife, let it be enough; he loathed himself for the state he was in over Anna. <Yet he was *not* satisfied. It was agony to know it.>"[44] Yet he allowed Tom to come to rest, as it were, in the very instability of his feelings—as in the added exclamatory sentence: "How rich and splendid his own life was, red and burning and blazing and sporting itself in the dark meshes of his body: and his wife, how she glowed and burned dark within her meshes! <Always it was so unfinished and unformed!>"[45] The final feeling is one of awe that the adventure of life is never concluded.

---

[42]Final Ms., pp. 196–97; M, p. 116; V, p. 124; P, pp. 128–29.

[43]Final Ms., p. 196; M, p. 116; V, p. 124; P, p. 129.

[44]Final Ms., p. 196; M, p. 116; V, p. 124; P, p. 129.

[45]Final Ms., p. 206; M, p. 123; V, p. 131; P, p. 135.

The Proofs

Yet Lawrence was not intent on profundities and solemnities to the exclusion of lighthearted or frivolous moments, as the humorous account of the wedding party in chapter 5 should demonstrate. Lawrence took some pains, for example, with the comical toasts of the tipsy and roisterous Brangwen men. Note how the rather coarse reference to a pigsty gives place to the vigorous but equally worldly "Hammer an' tongs":

Final Ms.	*Proof*
Kettle an' teapot, an' may you enjoy it.	Night an' day, an' may they enjoy it.
Bed an' blessing, and may you enjoy it. . . .	Hammer an' tongs, and may they enjoy it. . . .
Pig-sty an' pantry, an' may we enjoy it.	Bed an' blessin', an' may ye enjoy it.
Bed an' beauty, an' may we enjoy it.	Comin' and goin', an' may ye enjoy it.[46]

In the inconsequential stories of thistles ("angels") that form a comic diminuendo to Tom's drunken oratory, Lawrence delighted to add a telling detail:

'It's wonderful what children will get up their noses,' said Frank's wife. 'I c'n remember our Hemmie, she shoved one o' them bluebell things out o' th' middle of a bluebell, what they call "candles", up her nose, and oh we had some work! I'd seen her stickin' 'em on the end of her nose, like, but I never thought she'd be so soft as to shove

---

[46]Final Ms., pp. 208–9; M, p. 124; V, pp. 132–33; P, pp. 136–37.

From "The Sisters" to *The Rainbow*

it right up. She was a gel of eight or more. Oh my word, [what work—']< we got a crochet-hook an' I don't know what . . .'>[47]

Another benefit of noting the proof changes is that we can watch Lawrence capping a train of revision begun several drafts earlier. In the penultimate version of *The Rainbow*, Will had emerged as decidedly the weaker of the couple and the cause of Anna's abandonment of the Brangwen journey to the Promised Land. Unlike her balked husband, Anna finds at least partial fulfilment in childbearing; she is, in that measure, "Anna Victrix." Moreover, Will is blamed for failing to guide Anna into the New World, as Joseph guided Mary. Revising the proofs, however, Lawrence took much of the blame for the journey's end away from Will:

She should go also. But she could not go, when they called, because she must stay at home now. With a pang she relinquished the adventure to the unknown. She was bearing her children. And she knew that she could not go alone, save the man took her, as Joseph took Mary to Egypt. He would not take her. He could not rise up and depart for the unknown. His feet clung to the beloved earth of his home, he could not depart. So she must stay. (Final Ms., p. 301)

She should go also. But she could not go, when they called, because she must stay at home now. With satisfac-

[47]Final Ms., p. 213; M, p. 127; V, pp. 135–36; P, p. 139.

tion she relinquished the adventure to the unknown. She
was bearing her children. (Methuen proof, p. 181)

The revision makes Anna's relinquishment a natural outcome of her character; she is actually relieved to forsake the struggle onwards. And the revision was inevitable, because by the time Lawrence corrected the proofs he had added a new dimension to the second generation by enlarging chapter 8, in which Will becomes a quester leading Anna into new worlds of "Absolute Beauty."[48]

To stress Will's potential for independent action, Lawrence also altered descriptions of his uncouthness in social situations, which had seemed to be a mark of inadequacy. When Will and Anna visit Baron Skrebensky in the early version, the little baroness finds him "not quick enough" and "the wrong sort," with only the slightest feeling that he may be admirable in his own way.

Meanwhile the little baroness, with always a subtle light stirring in her full, lustrous, hazel eyes, was playing with Will Brangwen. He was not quick enough to [take her. He was the wrong sort for her, not subtle enough. She was rather bored. And yet she glanced again and again at his dark, living face, curiously, as if she wished she were like him, easy and unconscious as a full fire burning, burning without flickering. Herself, she was uneasy, twisting and

[48]Ross, "The Revisions of the Second Generation in *The Rainbow*," pp. 282–88.

From "The Sisters" to *The Rainbow*

restless as a ferret . . .]< see all her movements. Yet he watched her steadily, with unchanging, lit-up eyes. She was a strange creature to him. But she had no power over him. She flushed, and was irritated. Yet she glanced again and again at his dark, living face, curiously, as if she despised him. She despised his steady, warm, unironical nature, it had nothing for her. Yet it angered her as if she were jealous. He watched her with naive interest as he would watch a stoat playing. But he himself was not implicated. He was too stupid. She was all lambent, biting flames, he was a red fire burning steadily. She could get nothing out of him. So she made him flush darkly by assuming a biting, subtle class-superiority. He flushed, but still he did not understand. He was too stupid. >[49]

The revision accentuates the attractiveness and sufficiency of Will's nature, transforming his uncouthness into positive otherness. His unease at the tea table is not a sign of inadequacy but of strength; the baroness is "jealous" of his "unironical nature." Nevertheless, a note of social derogation remained, which Lawrence had to remove from the proofs. The repeated "He was too stupid" became "He was different in kind," and "He was too different"; and his "naive interest" in the baroness was changed to "deferential interest."[50] Thus the revisions increase Will's stature, asserting his positive difference in kind and the adequacy of his world.

---

[49]Original Ms., p. 297; Final Ms., p. 305; V, p. 196; P, p. 199.

[50]M, p. 185; V, p. 196; P, p. 199.

The Proofs

The evolution of the presentation of Mr. Harby, the autocratic headmaster of Brinsley St. School, is a unique example of unremitting and exploratory revision capped by proof changes. It is unique in two respects. First, it can be traced from the fragment of "The Wedding Ring" inserted into the original manuscript of *The Rainbow* through the drafts of the latter. Secondly, it comes from the most autobiographical episode in the novel, in which Lawrence drew directly on his own experiences as a schoolmaster; hence, it tested his artistic objectivity. We can watch the artist reliving the crises of the man and becoming, in the process, dispassionate master of them. In "The Wedding Ring," "Ella" simply hates Mr. Harby's one-dimensional personality: "He seemed to become something other than himself, in fulfilling the petty law of the school. She hated him bitterly as he stood, short and sturdy and like a bull dog, teaching her class for her. It seemed such a miserable thing for him to be doing . . . . Yet he used all himself, all his force and passion in the doing . . . . She hated him and felt brow-beaten by him, almost cowed."[51]

But the seeds of a more complex reaction are present: Does Harby use all himself or does he become something other than himself? So in the first (original) manuscript of *The Rainbow*, Ursula is "tormented by him": "He seemed to have some dev-

[51]Original Ms. (i.e., unrevised typescript), p. 568.

From "The Sisters" to *The Rainbow*

ilish office, dealing all in pin-pricks and little blows and twisting the joints of weaker children when fulfilling the law of the school. She was tormented by him bitterly as he stood . . . so unmanly and insulting to his own being . . . that he, a strong, powerful, man should use all his power for such a purpose, seemed almost indecent."[52]

Yet the melodramatic image of Harby as a medieval torturer still obscured the problem of a man divided against himself. Consequently, the final manuscript introduces the culprit in the form of Harby's will:

He seemed to have some sullen, stubborn, subdued will, that acquiesced in a task too small and petty for him, which yet, in a blind, passionate fury, he would fulfill, because he had set himself to it. . . . only this blind, dogged, wholesale will . . . always suppressing himself, till he was beside himself. Ursula suffered bitterly as he stood, short and handsome and powerful, teaching her class . . . threshing the trivial subject. It was habit with him now, to be so much less and meaner than his own nature. . . . The strange, genial light in his eyes was a vicious, cruel glint, his smile was one of torture. He was like a stallion kept up in a stall, fretted, and going mad.[53]

The disparity between Harby's will and his nature is caught in the verb "thresh" and also in the image of

[52]Ibid.
[53]Final Ms., pp. 580–81; M, pp. 362–63; V, pp. 387–88; P, pp. 387–88.

The Proofs

the fretted stallion. Subsequently in proof Lawrence cut much repetition, strengthened the animal image ("a strong creature tethered"), and added diagnosis: "He could not have a clear, pure purpose."[54] The final version transforms Ursula's reaction from simple hatred to empathy—"she suffered bitterly"— and deepens the analysis to expose the springs of his despotism in the willed choice of a job too mean and unexpressive for his nature.

As a last example we may observe that Lawrence did not fully justify the title of his novel until he rewrote its final paragraph in proof. There the beautiful and fitting symbol of the rainbow, spanning heaven and earth and prophesying a secular future as glorious as the biblical, finally rose to complete the "new architecture" of the novel:

[And the rainbow stood on her heart. She knew that the sordid people who crept hard-scaled and foul on the face of the earth's corruption were living still, that the rainbow was arched in their blood and would quiver to life in their passion, that with a cry of sorrow and repentance they would cast off their horny covering of self-care and self-conceit, that the scales would be broken and the horny rind burst asunder, that the new, clean, naked bodies would issue to a new germination, to a new growth, offered to the light and the wind and the clean rain, that the new growth should take place, the vast forest of mankind should spring up urgent and young out

---

[54]M, p. 363; V, pp. 387–88; P, pp. 387–88.

of the brittle, marshy foulness of the old corruption.]

< And the rainbow stood on the earth. She knew that the sordid people who crept hard-scaled and separate on the face of the world's corruption were living still, that the rainbow was arched in their blood and would quiver to life in their spirit, that they would cast off their horny covering of disintegration, that new clean, naked bodies would issue to a new germination, to a new growth, rising to the light and the wind and the clean rain of heaven. She saw in the rainbow the earth's new architecture, the old, brittle corruption of houses and factories swept away, the world built up in a living fabric of Truth, fitting to the over-arching heaven. >[55]

[55]Final Ms., p. 747; M, p. 463; V, p. 495; P, pp. 495–96.

CHAPTER 4

Vision and Revision in the Manuscripts

The final manuscript, unlike the proofs, was written and rewritten without a thought of truckling to unsympathetic editorial opinion. Lawrence's methods may be reconstructed from the strata of revisions; physical evidence leads to critical conclusions. The following textual history examines the physical state of the final manuscript in those places where irregularities have major textual consequences. It considers pagination; changes of paper, typewriter, and copy; marginal notes; and questions of transmission.

The size and brand of paper are of crucial importance. Throughout the final manuscript three brands of paper and four sizes of sheet were used. "Ryman's Linen Bank" appears in a uniform size, 9 and 15/16″ × 7 and 15/16″. The second brand, "Silver Linen," appears in three different sizes: 10″ × 7 and 13/16″ (type 1), 9 and 15/16″ × 8″ (type 2), and 10½″ × 8″ (type 3). The third brand has no watermark and measures 10½″ × 8″. We may express the placement of the three brands in the manuscript according to pagination, with references to the corresponding portions of the current Penguin and Viking texts:

Ryman's Linen Bank

Final Ms., pp. 1–159, 220–309, 389–419
Penguin, pp. 7–105, 144–202, 261–82
Viking, pp. 1–101, 140–99, 259–80

Silver Linen, type 1

Final Ms., pp. 160–219, 315–42, 356–88, 509–58
Penguin, pp. 105–43, 207–27, 240–60, 340–73
Viking, pp. 101–39, 205–24, 237–58, 339–73

Silver Linen, type 2

Final Ms., pp. 310–14, 343–55
Penguin, pp. 202–7, 227–39
Viking, pp. 199–204, 224–36

Silver Linen, type 3

Final Ms., pp. 420–90/499,* 595–747
Penguin, pp. 283–333, 397–496
Viking, pp. 281–332, 397–495

No Watermark

Final Ms., pp. 500–508, 559–94
Penguin, pp. 334–40, 373–97
Viking, pp. 333–39, 373–97

---

*See footnote 1.

Vision and Revision in the Manuscripts

The areas of significant textual irregularity comprise two units of composition of some complexity and three cases of simple excision.

The first such compositional unit comprises pages 310–88—that is, most of chapter 7 and all of chapters 8 and 9. Pages 310–14, describing Will and Anna in Lincoln Cathedral, and pages 343–55, describing Will's flirtation with Jennie and his sensual revels with Anna at the end of chapter 8, are handwritten insertions on Silver Linen type 2. Thus the two holograph insertions were written on exactly the same type of paper, which is a distinctly different type of Silver Linen from that used in bulk for the rest of the manuscript. The obvious deduction is that the two holograph portions probably were written and inserted at the same time. Moreover, the probability of contemporaneous composition is increased by the fact that the latter passage clearly makes use of a motif from the former to achieve consonance. Will and Anna's sensual experience of "Absolute Beauty" is compared to the "absolute beauty of the round arch" in the cathedral. Indeed, a sentence later deleted from the proofs shows that Lawrence had the analogy in mind when composing. As Will held Jennie the warehouse lass, "He forgot all time and space, as in the cathedral."[2]

Pages 315–19 have "secondary" numbers 9

---

[1]The awkward 490/499 number was caused by repagination; it does not indicate a break in the text.

[2]Final Ms., p. 346.

From "The Sisters" to *The Rainbow*

through 13 typed in the upper left-hand corner.[3] It would seem, then, that handwritten pages 310–14 were copied from the missing eight pages of typescript (i.e. pages with secondary numbering 1–8). Therefore, what must have been a heavily revised section, to judge by surrounding sections, has been revised again in the holograph insertion.[4] That is, we may assume that between the original and final versions the manuscript passed through another stage which has not been preserved. As corroboratory evidence, the hypothetical word count of the missing pages (secondary numbers 1–8) roughly tallies with the word count on pp. 310–14; and the handwriting is exceptionally small and flawless, indicating that Lawrence was copying from another version.

The portions of the final manuscript surrounding the second holograph insertion also have secondary numbering. Pages 321–42 are numbered 2–23 and pages 356–88 are numbered 1–33. In fact, the numbering of pages 239–490, done by hand in both pencil and ink, is very makeshift. From the letter to Ottoline Morrell we know that Lawrence himself lost

---

[3]In a letter to Ottoline Morrell, Lawrence asks her to correct his random numbering by using "secondary numbering" (*CL*, pp. 335–36). I adapt his term to include the alternative numbering of the typists as well as the alternative handwritten numbers.

[4]See original Ms., pp. 299–313.

Vision and Revision in the Manuscripts

count, starting a batch "at 250 at random" (*CL*, p. 335). Lawrence's slip is understandable because he was receiving batches of typescript from two different typists;[5] excising and inserting, and sending them on to Ottoline Morrell. The letter also implies that Ottoline may have done some, if not all, of the numbering in pencil.

Having established these facts, we can account for the secondary numbering as a necessary part of the compositional unit. Pages 315–42 and 356–88 surround the handwritten insertion, pages 343–55, that ends chapter 8. In the original manuscript this culminating experience in the marriage of Will and Anna occupies a mere three pages. Thus the holograph insertion of twelve pages represents a great expansion and revision. The fluid state of the text presented the typist, who wanted to keep order in her typescript without the aid of normal pagination, with a serious dilemma. Viola Meynell's solution was to type secondary numbers in the left-hand corner simply as a way of maintaining sequence within the batches.

The entire unit witnesses to the many stages of revision through which the text passed. Certainly in the case of pages 310–14, and probably in that of pages 343–55, the work passed through four creative

---

[5]In addition, Eleanor Farjeon, a friend of Viola Meynell, asserts that she too helped with the typing of the manuscript (Nehls, ed., *Lawrence*, I, 305).

From "The Sisters" to *The Rainbow*

stages: (1) the original manuscript, which was heavily revised; (2) a postulated first version of the final manuscript, probably also revised, to judge by the heavy revision in surrounding portions of the final manuscript; (3) the holograph insertion, probably replacing eight typed pages and perhaps containing further revision; (4) a proof stage.

The second compositional unit consists of pages 509–58, corresponding to Penguin pp. 340–72 (or most of chapter 12 and one third of chapter 13). A note on the back of page 495 of the original manuscript indicates that Viola Meynell, the principal typist, farmed out chapter 11 to be typed by a Miss K. Lee.[6] A change in typewriter and paper at page 420 of the final manuscript corroborates the note. Moreover, pages 420–508 and 559–747 of the final manuscript were typed on the same machine and, with the exception of pages 500–508 and 559–94, on the same paper, Silver Linen type 3. Finally, the exceptional unwatermarked paper only appears in the portion of the typescript prepared on the second typewriter, presumably that of Miss Lee. The deduction follows that Miss Lee typed pages 420–747, except for the fifty-page block, 509–58. This block, typed by Miss Meynell on the same machine she used for pages 1–419, is a retyped version of the previous,

---

[6]Original Ms., p. 495 verso: "Miss Viola Meynell 2a Granville Place Portman Square W. From Miss K. Lee. 120 Welldon Crescent. Harrow."

discarded block. In the first place, page 559 does not run on; Lawrence deleted one and one-fourth lines at the top of the page to make the transition from page 558. Secondly, revision has been made between the original and the final manuscripts. The revisions are neatly typed into this portion of the final manuscript, with no sign of the handwritten revision evident in surrounding portions. This accounts for the clean appearance of pages 509-58—there is hardly a mark except spelling and punctuation corrections. But although there was undoubtedly revision, the length of the block was not much altered. By comparing the original manuscript with the final, we see that Lawrence made a great number of precise verbal changes which, however, barely affected the length. He altered significantly his method of describing industry, departing from the style of *Sons and Lovers* and moving toward that of *Women in Love*. In the Wiggiston section of *The Rainbow*, Lawrence marks the historical turning point when the industrial machine began to run on purely mechanical and antihuman principles. In revision he accentuated the hellishness of modern industry and the complete disappearance of the compromise between rural England and the collieries that he had described in *Sons and Lovers* and the early short stories. His technique was to repeat throughout the scene a sort of check list of evocative adjectives, like "amorphous," "chaotic," "rigid," and "mathematical." For example, Uncle Tom's library gives

From "The Sisters" to *The Rainbow*

[a rare sense of leisure and holiday to the idlers who loitered before its windows] <the same sense of hard, mechanical activity, activity mechanical yet inchoate, and> looking out on the hideous abstraction of the town . . . and at the great, [stately] <mathematical> colliery on the other side.

He looked round at the red [disarray, the unmanageable small]<chaos, the rigid, amorphous> confusion of Wiggiston.[7]

The third area of textual irregularity consists of three cases of excision. In the first two cases Lawrence had second thoughts about unnecessary elaboration, cropping a total of six pages that had already been typed as part of the final manuscript. He excised pages 479, 479[bis], 480, and 481 of the original manuscript between pages 478–79 of the final manuscript, and pages 488–89 of the original between pages 484–85 of the final. The discarded passages elaborated on a theme already overworked in the chapter, deriding Christians for interpreting the Scriptures in a materialistic, democratic way.

The third instance of excision is most important. Lawrence cropped a long interior monologue of Ursula (pages 634–38 in the original manuscript).[8] Though turgid and repetitious, the monologue anticipates the argument of *The Crown* essays and

[7]Final Ms., pp. 519, 523; M, pp. 323–24, 326; V, pp. 345, 348; P, pp. 346, 349.

[8]The monologue would have come on V, p. 441, and P, p. 441.

Vision and Revision in the Manuscripts

several passages in *Women in Love*. The idea came to him late in the writing of the original manuscript, and on returning to it in revision he must have realized that its implications would take him beyond the conceptual bounds of *The Rainbow*. Its presence in the early draft, however, points to the nature of Lawrence's creativity. His second thoughts on the appropriateness of such undramatic speculation in fiction and his later use of the ideas in philosophical discourse (i.e., *The Crown*) demonstrate that art-speech preceded didactic speech during "The Sisters" project. The essays grew out of challenges and obscurities found in the process of writing fiction.

Thus the manuscripts resemble successive palimpsests. The common notion of Lawrence as a romantic artist who scorned niggling revision but, when displeased with his work, started again from scratch is truthful only insofar as it implies that Lawrence did not revise in a piecemeal or haphazard fashion. His practice, in fact, is similar to that of the ideal poet envisaged in T. S. Eliot's essay "Tradition and the Individual Talent." Eliot, of course, is talking about the whole of Western literature, but he implies a quality of mind that Lawrence exemplifies perfectly: "The existing order is complete before the new work arrives; for order to persist after the supervention of novelty, the *whole* existing order must be, if ever so slightly, altered; and so the relations, proportions, values of each work of art toward the whole are readjusted; and this is conformity between the old and the new."⁹ By substituting "intuition" for "new work," we get a fair generalization for Lawrence's practice.

In the space available, I want to give a rather full example of Lawrence's grasp of the "living rhythm of the whole work" that informs even the most minute, local revisions.¹⁰ The love scenes that take place in natural settings and under the aegis of the moon provide a striking illustration of Lawrence's habitual practice in revision.

Scenic echoing is the great and pervasive technical innovation of the novel, binding it together at every level—narrative, thematic, and verbal. One advantage of the method is that the reader is always making comparisons, registering personal and historical change, vividly aware in any one moment of the different fates of the three generations. The revisions of both original and final manuscripts show Lawrence gradually realizing the full potential of the comparative technique. For instance, it was not until he had written the final love contests between Ursula and Skrebensky in chapter 15 that he saw clearly the strategy of having analogous moments of passion in each generation, so that the increasing difficulty of achieving a viable love relationship would be recorded in the progressive deformation of

---

⁹T. S. Eliot, *The Sacred Wood* (London: Methuen, 1920, rpt. 1969), p. 50.

¹⁰Lawrence, *Phoenix*, p. 313.

common verbal and passional rhythms. The impetus for rewriting was the need to build up to the culminating sexual encounters of chapter 15; but Lawrence saw that one scenic alteration would require that "the *whole* existing order must be, if ever so slightly, altered." Consequently, the order of revision of the similar love scenes was:

1. Original manuscript: Ursula and Skrebensky on the Lincolnshire coast, chapter 15

2. Original manuscript, revised: Will and Anna stacking corn, chapter 4

3. Final manuscript, revised: Ursula and Skrebensky in the Stackyard, chapter 11

The ferocious encounters in chapter 15 function as the culmination of a relationship that has degenerated into mere willed sexuality. After nearly completing the original manuscript, Lawrence finally fashioned a vocabulary and scenic structure capable of presenting the psychic turbulence of modern man and woman. The diction of this chapter is remarkable, especially when one considers that the Stackyard scene in chapter 11 was a relatively slight affair in the original manuscript. It stresses the inhuman or elemental qualities of the lovers' responses. Ursula "vibrated like a jet of electric, firm fluid"; she craves the "salt, burning" passion of the sea; "she was like metal"; she lies after consummation with a "rigid face, like metal in the moonlight." Her kiss is "hard, rending," and Skrebensky feels himself "fusing down to nothingness . . . his heart melted in fear." Even more strikingly, the scene is conceived as a predatory contest of attack and counterattack. Skrebensky takes her in order to be "savagely satisfied . . . revenged"; and Ursula, who "prowled" like a "possessed creature," grapples him to her "till he gave way as if dead."

The trouble was that the technical and thematic inspiration of chapter 15 broke too abruptly and stridently on the surface of the original version. The imaginative distance between the mild love duel of Will and Anna in chapter 4 and the murderous duel in chapter 15 was so great as to be incomprehensible. The inspiration was proving a danger as well as a boon by threatening to make the experience of chapter 15 simply discontinuous with that of earlier generations. So Lawrence went back to the second generation and explored analogous love scenes in the light of his maturing vision and with the freshly tapped verbal and structural resources of chapter 15.

He had created in the original version of chapter 4 the activity of cornstacking as a dramatic correlative for the passion of Will and Anna. Now, without marring the delicacy of the scene, he worked to deepen its significance as an initiation, an expression of the unknown, a ritual of self-discovery. First he strengthened the symbolic role of the moon that presides over the scene as it had over the beach in chapter 15. The moon becomes for Anna, as for Tom and Ursula, the symbol of the unknown be-

Vision and Revision in the Manuscripts

yond human life with which she desires communion. As the work of cornstacking imparts a rhythm to the pursuit and retreat of the lovers, so the moon imparts a psychic rhythm—"laying bare her bosom" and making her "drift and ebb like a wave":

She took her new two sheaves and [started a new stack. And as she turned away towards the moon which always furrowed its hands in her bosom, she saw him rise from stooping over the earth, she saw him coming towards her. He was unexperienced, it took him longer to make his sheaves stand up.] < walked towards him, as he rose from stooping over the earth. He was coming out of the near distance. She set down her sheaves to make a new stook. They were unsure. Her hands fluttered. Yet she broke away, and turned to the moon, which laid bare her bosom, so she felt as if her bosom were the sea heaving and panting with moonlight. And he had to put up her two sheaves, which fell down. He worked in silence. The rhythm of the work carried him away again, as she was coming near. >[11]

The revisions were inspired by the incandescent moon of chapter 15 that had "laid bare" Skrebensky's chest and witnessed Ursula's "salt, bitter passion of the sea." They inspired, in turn, the revisions of the second stackyard scene in chapter 11, in which Ursula's "body opened wide like a quivering anemone" to the "great white moon." And the

---

[11]Original Ms., p. 182; M, p. 110; V, pp. 117–19; P, p. 122.

revised scene ends as it began, with a vision of the moon echoing the "high moon, liquid-brilliant" that Tom noticed after proposing to Lydia: "He looked through her hair at the moon, which seemed to swim liquid-bright."

But Lawrence's main effort went into the climax of the scene, when Will's "deep-sounding will" succeeds in bringing Anna to him. The passage describing the rapturous kiss was wholly rewritten:

The kiss lasted, there among the moonlight [till he wanted her. He wanted her exceedingly. They stood there enfolded, hanging in the balance. It was pain to him that he wanted her. It was a new thing to him. He had never wanted her, he had never wanted any woman before. His wanting her seemed to separate them. It hurt him.]<. He kissed her again and she kissed him. And again they were kissing together. Till something happened in him, he was strange. He wanted her. He wanted her exceedingly. She was something new. They stood there folded, suspended in the night. And his whole being quivered with surprise, as from a blow. He wanted her, and he wanted to tell her so. But the shock was too great to him. He had never realised before. She had a face, she had hands and feet and soft dresses, but one could not want her. Yet now he did want her. He trembled with initiation and unusedness, he did not know what to do. He held her more gently, gently, much more gently. And he was glad, and breathless, and almost in tears. But he knew he wanted her. Something fixed in him for ever. In his heart she was his wife. And he was very glad, and afraid. He did not know what to do, as they stood there in the open, moonlit field.

Vision and Revision in the Manuscripts

He looked through her hair at the moon, which seemed to swim liquid-bright. >[12]

Their kiss has become a transcendent experience, a death of their normal selves: hence, he "quivered" as from a "blow," as Ursula "quivered as if she were being destroyed" in the arms of Skrebensky.[13] The sudden birth of a primal self is conveyed by "strange" and "surprise," and the complex feelings of joy and fear: "He was glad, and afraid." A subsequent stroke in the final manuscript explicitly evoked birth — "'Anna' he said in wonder and [rapture] <birth-pain>" — by echoing Tom's "new birth" in the first generation: "He returned gradually, but newly created, as after a gestation, a new birth, in the womb of darkness."[14]

The prose rhythms also gained in revision as Lawrence made the repetition mimetic rather than tiresome, the phrase "He wanted her" punctuating Will's thoughts rhythmically and not monotonously. The revised rhythms lend an air of impersonality and inevitability to the encounter. In fact, the passage is a prime example of the emergence of Lawrence's mature prose style, composed of short sentences that overlap and repeat impressions with

---

[12]Original Ms., pp. 185–86. In the final Ms., p. 190, the passage was slightly altered and condensed. Again, in proof one sentence was altered and another added: see M, p. 112; V, p. 120; P, p. 124.

[13]V, p. 446; P, p. 446.

[14]V, p. 41; P, p. 46.

slight but significant variation. And although he expanded greatly, he was capable of trimming: he cut from the final manuscript the lame sentences "She had a face, she had hands and feet and soft dresses, but one could not want her. Yet he did want her."

Turning to the Stackyard scene in chapter 11, then, Lawrence thoroughly revised the love duel so as to reflect the violent and even murderous potential in the relationship of Ursula and Skrebensky that he had discovered while writing chapter 15. Once more the moon is a presiding presence. But now it is a moon of fiercely inhuman aspect, not simply apart from but opposed to "this temporary warm world," as Lawrence emphasized: "Looking away, she saw the delicate glint of oats dangling from the side of the stack, in the moonlight, something proud and royal, [along with her,] <and quite impersonal. She was proud with them, where they were, she also. But in this temporary warm world of the commonplace, she was a kind, good girl.>"[15] The dance in the moonlit field is transformed into a contest of wills. Skrebensky, who has initiated the contest, becomes a more formidable and hostile opponent; he would "compel" her and frustrate her communion with the moon:

---

[15]Final Ms., p. 475. In proof "She was proud with them, where they were, she also" became "She had been proud with them, where they were, she had been also" (M, p. 301; V, p. 321; P, p. 323).

Vision and Revision in the Manuscripts

[Only she liked the supple run of his movement upon her, warm and dark and attached like clothing to her. And he exerted all his power to warm her to him. She liked him, but she remained scarcely softened.

He was mad with passion for her firm, cool body, that was compact of brilliance like the moon itself. His muscles set in tension upon her, he could not relax. He must have her entirely — entirely.]

< She liked the dance: it eased her, put her into a sort of trance. But it was only a kind of waiting, of using up the time that intervened between her and her pure being. She left herself against him, she let him exert all his power over her, as if he would gain power over her, to bear her down. She received all the force of his power. She even triumphed in it. She was cold and unmoved as a pillar of salt.

His will was set and straining with all its tension to encompass her and compel her. If he could only compel her. He seemed to be annihilated. She was cold and hard and compact of brilliance as the moon itself, and beyond him as the moonlight was beyond him, never to be grasped or known. If he could only set a bond round her and compel her! > [16]

The predatory quality of their lust here reaches an extreme of mere destructiveness. Skrebensky hunts Ursula; and she counters with a murderous defense: "And she seemed to agree. She was bright as a piece

---

[16] Final Ms., p. 472. In proof "She even triumphed in it" became "She even wished he might overcome her" (M, p. 298; V, p. 318; P, p. 320).

From "The Sisters" to *The Rainbow*

of the moon, as if she were mad.

"Don't you like me to-night?" repeated the soft voice.

And she knew that if she turned, she ~~could tear him to pieces,~~ *would die. A strange rage filled her, a rage to tear living things asunder. Her hands felt like teaning, like metal* ~~scatter his shadow in fragments under the moonlight.~~ *blades of destruction.*

"Let me alone," she said.
Darkness, an obstinacy settled on him too, on a kind of inertia.
A ~~numbers madness and determination came over him too.~~ He sat ~~just~~ ~~days beside her.~~ She threw off her cloak and walked towards the moon, silver-white herself. He followed her closely.

The music began again and the dance. He appropriated her. There was a fierce, white, cold passion in her heart. But he held her close, *always present, like a soft weight upon her, bearing her down,* and danced with her. ~~Supple, supple, and insinuating~~ was his body against her as they ~~as they~~ danced. He held her very close, so that she could feel his body, *the weight of him sinking, settling upon her, overbearing* ~~his breast, his belly, his legs pressing warm~~ *her life and energy, making her exert along with him,* ~~and insinuating upon her,~~ she felt his hands pressing behind her, upon her. But ~~between his~~ *still in* her body was ~~burning~~ *the subdued, cold, indomitable* ~~defence, cold~~ passion, *She liked the dance. it eased her, put her into a sort of trance. But it was only a kind* ~~Only she liked the supple run of his movement upon her, warm and dark~~ *of waiting, of ~~~~ using ~~~~ time that intervened between her and her pure being. She left herself* ~~and attached like ~~~~ to her. And he exerted all his power to~~ *against him, she let him exert all his power over her, as if ~~~~ he would gain power over her, to bear* ~~warm her to him. She liked him, but she remained scarcely softened.~~ *her down. She received all the power of his power. She even triumphed in it. She was cold and unmoved as a pillar of salt.* ~~He was mad with passion for her firm, cool body, that was compact~~ *his will was set and straining with all its tension to compass her and compel her.* ~~If he could only compel her. He seemed to be annihilated,~~ ~~both~~ *She was ~~~~ cold and hard* ~~of brilliance like the moon itself. His ~~~~ set in tension upon~~ *and ~~~~ brilliant as the moon itself, and beyond him in the moonlight ~~~~ was ~~~~ like, never to be grasped.* ~~her, he could not relax. He must have her entirely — entirely.~~ *If he could only set a brand round her and compel her.*

So they danced four or five dances, always together, always his *his body more subtle, pulsing,* will ~~~~ becoming more tense, ~~bending like iron~~ upon her. And still he had not got her, she was hard and ~~compact~~ *bright* as ever, But he *intact.* must weave himself round her, enclose her, enclose her. ~~Then he would~~ *in a net of shadow, of darkness, so she would be like a bright creature gleaming in a net of shadows. Caught. Then he would*

Page 472 of the final manuscript of *The Rainbow*. (Courtesy of the Humanities Research Library, University of Texas at Austin.)

Vision and Revision in the Manuscripts

Page 473 of the final manuscript of *The Rainbow*. (Courtesy of the Humanities Research Library, University of Texas at Austin).

From "The Sisters" to the *The Rainbow*

of moonlight, as bright as a steel blade, he seemed to be clasping a steel blade. Yet he would clasp her, if it killed him."[17]

The revised passages rely on a strikingly poetic and impersonal vocabulary, inspired by chapter 15 but extended far beyond the resources of the original manuscript. Ursula is not only "a pillar of salt," she is also "cold," "corrosive," a "poison," "deadly," a "blade" or "knife" of destruction. She has the fierce clarity of the moon, and the "glimmering," "bluish-steely" fires of the stacks. Skrebensky, on the other hand, is described as "dross," "soft iron," a "dead magnetic stone," and (most tellingly) "inert." Under the great "moon-conflagration" he appears "shadowy," "unreal," and "wavering." The scrupulously physical diction anatomizes the effects of their straining wills: "[She felt him, like a black shadow, wanting to draw close to her. Whilst she wanted the brightness and the brilliance of the moon.] < Skrebensky, like a barren stone, weighed on her, the weight of his presence detained her. She felt the burden of him, the blind, persistent, inert burden. He was inert, and he weighed upon her. > "[18] Ursula's feeling of being borne down is conveyed by the verbal activity of sinking, lapsing into inertia, and so

[17] Final Ms., p. 473. In proof "he seemed to be clasping a steel blade" became "he seemed to be clasping a blade that hurt him" (M, p. 299; V, p. 319; P, pp. 320-21).

[18] Final Ms., p. 471. In proof "barren stone" became "loadstone" (M, p. 298; V, p. 317; P, p. 319).

Vision and Revision in the Manuscripts

on. Similarly, at the climax of the struggle, Ursula's destruction of Skrebensky is given as the end result of physical processes, which are enumerated in the verbs:

Till gradually his warm, [supple shadow] <soft iron> yielded, yielded, and she was there fierce, [blazing fierce and hard and cold upon him, and his heart was gone, and his strength. Under her hard, open-mouthed, coldly fierce kiss he succumbed, and she held him there, the victim.] <corrosive, seething with his destruction, seething like some horrible, corrosive salt around the last substance of his being, destroying him, destroying him in the kiss. And her soul screamed with triumph, and his soul was silent with agony and annihilation. So she held him there, the victim, shrivelled, bloodless, like an infinitely shrivelled corpse. She had triumphed: he was not anymore.>[19]

So attentive was Lawrence to the demands of the method that in proof he substituted physical verbs where the revised conception was clumsily melodramatic: "Her soul [screamed] <crystallized> with triumph"; "his soul was [silent] <dissolved> with agony"; and "[shrivelled, bloodless . . . corpse] <consumed, annihilated>."[20]

The purpose of the cumulative revisions is to describe the impersonal forces that operate below the surface of normal human consciousness. The

---
[19] Final Ms., p. 474.
[20] M, p. 300; V, p. 320; P, p. 322.

scene is the most deliberate and highly mannered rendering in all of Lawrence's fiction of the primal ego underlying the superficial "old stable ego — of character" (*CL*, p. 282).

Part Two

From "The Sisters" to *Women in Love*

CHAPTER 5

The Manuscripts: Three Preliminary Drafts

The history of the composition of *Women in Love* is even more complicated than that of *The Rainbow*. In the first place, the novel remained in typescript for five years. Intimidated by the banning of *The Rainbow* and repeated threats of libel suits from Lady Ottoline Morrell and Philip Heseltine, publishers would not venture to handle the sequel to *The Rainbow*. The novel went the round of publishers and was refused by Methuen, Duckworth, Unwin, and private publishers like Cecil Palmer and C. W. Beaumont. Even Lawrence's agent, J. B. Pinker, silently agreed with the generally adverse opinion and did not actively support the novel.[1] Before Lawrence began the thorough revision of the

---

[1] When Lawrence discovered several years later that Pinker had not circulated the three copies of the typescript in his possession, ignoring Lawrence's instruction to send copies to prospective publishers, he transferred his business to Martin Secker. See *CL*, p. 618. Lawrence negotiated personally with Secker and Seltzer about *Women in Love*, asking Secker not to mention the new publishing scheme to Pinker. See *Letters from Lawrence to Secker*, p. 13.

final draft of *Women in Love*, he knew that there was no hope of finding a publisher in the foreseeable future: "I have done a novel which nobody will print, after *The Rainbow* experience. It has been the round of publishers by now, and rejected by all" (*CL*, pp. 504–5). It speaks for Lawrence's dedication to his art that he persevered in "one of the labours of Hercules"[2] — drafting and revising over a period of three and one-half years — when he knew that the novel was unlikely to find a public.

Yet Lawrence did pass the various typescripts of the novel among a small circle of friends and admirers, from whom he sought opinion and advice. As he wrote to Catherine Carswell, who was reading a draft with her husband, Donald: "I am glad you liked the novel — thanks for the suggestions."[3] One of the surviving typescripts has marginal suggestions signed "D. C." (Donald Carswell), some of which Lawrence followed when revising. The fact that the typescripts were circulating for such a long time and undergoing periodic revisions means that the task of establishing a chronology of composition is difficult.

Nor do the published selections of Lawrence's letters reveal much of the process of composition. The scholar must search in dozens of public and private collections for the unpublished letters that sup-

---

[2] Lawrence to Amy Lowell, 12 Oct. 1916, Harvard University Library.

[3] Huxley, ed., *Letters*, p. 382.

plement and clarify the public record.[4] Given such handicaps, it is small wonder that previous attempts to reconstruct the compositional history have been either truncated or wrong.[5]

Fortunately the surviving manuscript materials are extensive. These are, in chronological order:

1. Two early fragments which Kinkead-Weekes has entitled "Sisters I" and "Sisters II." Composed in 1913. Roberts lists these as E441b.

2. Two chapters from an early draft, published by George Ford as "Prologue to *Women in Love*," *Texas Quarterly*, 6 (1963), 98–111, and "'The Wedding Chapter' of D. H. Lawrence's *Women in Love*," *Texas Studies in Language and Literature*, 6 (1964), 134–47. Composed in 1916. Roberts, E441c.

3. Ten exercise books in holograph, containing

---

[4] Harry T. Moore's *Collected Letters*, like Huxley's pioneer volume, does not include a good number of letters that discuss the progress of the novel. To supplement the Moore and Huxley editions, see the two volumes of Lawrence's correspondence with Martin Secker, *Letters from a Publisher* (London: Enitharmon Press, 1970) and *Letters from Lawrence to Secker*; and Gerald M. Lacy, ed., *Letters to Thomas and Adele Seltzer* (Santa Barbara, Calif.: Black Sparrow Press, 1976).

[5] See the following treatments: Herbert Davis, "*Women in Love*: A Corrected Typescript"; George Ford, *Double Measure* (New York: Holt, Rinehart and Winston, 1965), pp. 164–66; Kinkead-Weekes, p. 399; Emile Delavenay, letter to *TLS*, Jan. 1, 1970, p. 12.

The dispersal of manuscripts has misled several scholars whose erroneous speculations have reached a wide audience.

From "The Sisters" to *Women in Love*

the last one-third of the typescript, from the point where Lawrence abandoned composing on the typewriter. Composed in 1916. Roberts, E441a.

4. Two duplicate typescripts with extensive holograph revisions.[6] These began as a typescript and its carbon copy but were shuffled by Lawrence during revision. Composed in 1916. Roberts lists one of the duplicates as E441d, but not the other, which is owned by the University of Toronto.

5. One typescript with extensive holograph revisions, which was made from one of the antecedent typescripts and from which both Seltzer and Secker

---

Herbert Davis was the first to describe the typescript now owned by the University of Toronto. Unaware that a later typescript of the novel existed, he mistakenly ascribed any differences between the Toronto typescript and the published book to changes in the proof sheets, which were not printed until 1920. More seriously, Emile Delavenay has asserted that "there is no factual evidence that suggests any substantial modification by Lawrence to the final draft of *Women in Love* after . . . November 7, 1916." This is a demonstrably false assertion. As we shall see, the factual evidence amply proves that Lawrence revised not only the draft of 7 Nov. but also a subsequent draft and that he did not finish work on the last draft until Sept. 1919, almost three years later than Delavenay asserts he finished.

[6] In the collection of the Humanities Research Library of the University of Texas at Austin, this typescript is called the "original manuscript," the subsequent typescript the "definitive manuscript." For clarity of exposition, I shall call the antecedent, or "original" typescript, the *penultimate draft* and the subsequent, or "definitive" typescript, the *final draft*.

The Manuscripts

set up their first editions. Composed 1917–19. Roberts, E441e.

The sequence of composition seems to have been as follows. After the publication of *The Rainbow* in September 1915, Lawrence worked at essays. During the autumn he revised the Italian and German studies that became *Twilight in Italy* and composed six essays, later published as *The Crown*, for *The Signature* magazine. On first moving to Cornwall in January 1916, he continued to write "philosophy": "I am writing myself a little book of philosophy" (*CL*, p. 408). By 25 February he sent Lady Ottoline Morrell "the destructive half" of his philosophy, probably the unfinished work called "Goats and Compasses" in Philip Heseltine's prospectus for "The Rainbow Books and Music."[7] Lady Ottoline did not find the philosophy sympathetic, for Lawrence wrote to her on 15 March 1916: "Never mind that you don't like my philosophy: it doesn't matter. I am writing nothing just at present. I shall begin when we are settled in our cottage: but I am not quite sure what I shall do. If I can get a manuscript from Germany, I shall go on with that. It is a novel I began three years ago. I should like to go on with it now."[8] The manuscript

---

[7] See my argument in "*Goats and Compasses* and/or *Women in Love*: A Critical Exchange," *D. H. Lawrence Review*, 6 (1973), 33–46.

[8] Lawrence to Ottoline Morrell, Humanities Research Library.

Writing to Bertrand Russell, Lady Ottoline could be bru-

From "The Sisters" to *Women in Love*

in Germany was "The Insurrection of Miss Houghton," which did not finally reach Lawrence until after the war when he rewrote it as *The Lost Girl*.[9] Thus Lawrence did not immediately decide to continue the story of "The Sisters." For a time he considered starting again on "The Insurrection," whose style he described as "quite unlike my usual style — more eventual" (*CL*, p. 616).

Lawrence made the decision to work again on the material of "The Sisters" in late April 1916. The first draft came "rushing out" making him feel "very triumphant" (*CL*, p. 455). By May 1916 he could announce that "I have married Ursula — yesterday. Two-thirds of the novel are written" (*CL*, p. 454); and on 30 June he had "finished *The Sisters*, in effect" (*CL*, p. 457) except for a last chapter that he would write "some time, when one's heart is not so contracted" (*CL*, p. 461). Deciding to type the holograph draft himself because "we have got no money," he asked Kot to send him a typewriter ribbon. But he began on 12 July 1916 with a worn ribbon on the same Smith-Corona typewriter he had used for the opening pages of *The Rainbow* original manuscript, making a carbon copy as he went along. On 21 July he told Pinker that he would send

---

tally frank about her displeasure: "It is dreadful stuff — bad in *every* way. I feel so sorry & miserable about it. It is rubbish. A child of Frieda's" (Sandra Jobson Darroch, *Ottoline* [New York: Coward, McCann & Geoghegan, 1975]), p. 169n.

[9] Ford, *Double Measure*, pp. 41-42.

the manuscript to be typed in his office and that he was "scribbling out the final draft" (*CL*, p. 469). Four-fifths of the novel were completed.

But the typing proved to be much more than a simple copying of the holograph. He began instead to compose on the typewriter which, he reported to Amy Lowell, "runs so glibly, and has at last become a true confrère."[10] The novel was changing and expanding radically under his hand, for on 9 September 1916 he told the impatient Pinker that it was "only half-done as yet."[11] He had "recomposed all the first part on the typewriter."[12] The labor was both obsessive and exhausting, as he complained: "I only want to finish this novel, which is like a malady or a madness while it lasts. It will take only a week or two" (*CL*, p. 475). In fact, it took a good deal longer because his poor health, further debilitated by the nervous strain of typing, forced him to abandon the typing on 13 October, when the novel was two-thirds completed.[13] At that point he had typed 368 pages, or fully 22 chapters.[14] He composed the remaining

---

[10] Nehls, *Lawrence*, I, 389–90.

[11] Lawrence to Pinker, in possession of Forster.

[12] Lawrence to Pinker, 20 Jan. 1917, in possession of Forster.

[13] See Lawrence to Mrs. Clayton, 13 Oct. 1916: "This typing is bad for me . . . it upsets me and hurts my nerves, so I give it up." Nottingham Public Library.

[14] At the top of page one of the first Exercise Book, Lawrence has written "continued from p. 368 (type)"; and the holograph page does indeed correspond to p. 368 of the penultimate draft.

From "The Sisters" to *Women in Love*

one-third in a series of ten small exercise books. Actually, textual evidence suggests that this last one-third was the corresponding part of the third draft, corrected by the ailing Lawrence but not written afresh.[15] In either case, he sent the exercise books on 25 and 31 October to be typed in Pinker's office, and Pinker promptly returned the "first part of the typed ms." on 6 November and the rest shortly thereafter.[16]

The physical states of the duplicate typescripts supplement the incomplete testimony of the letters. Pinker had followed Lawrence's practice, preparing two copies of the last one-third of the novel. So Lawrence had two complete duplicate typescripts by the second week of November. The duplicates, as we have them, are "composite" in the sense that they consist of both ribbon copy and carbon copy, apparently put together in a haphazard manner. Usually whole chapters are either one or the other, but sometimes a small number of pages, or even single pages, have been alternated. Both duplicates show extensive revisions, made at different times and by different hands. The University of Toronto typescript can be distinguished from the Texas one by the increased appearance of Frieda Lawrence's hand in the interlinear revisions.

The revision of these duplicates was done in

---

[15]See p. 112.
[16]Lawrence to Pinker, Lockwood Memorial Library.

stages.[17] Lawrence first made a preliminary run-through in both, changing a few words or a sentence here and there. Next he returned to the beginning and made extensive revisions that Frieda copied into the corresponding duplicate portions. Finally, when the pages had been gathered into complete typescripts, he added slight revisions to the one that he sent to Pinker.

Many of the textual peculiarities of the typescripts can be explained by the haste with which Lawrence prepared them and the sheer quantity of the revisions. He revised the completed typescripts thoroughly and at top speed, probably by 21 November 1916: "Revising it, I do admire it. But I am not everybody."[18] He was anxious to prepare the duplicates as quickly as possible: one to be read by friends like Catherine and Donald Carswell whose opinion he valued and the other to circulate among publishers. Incredible as it seems, he must have completed the substantial revisions and corrections of the typescripts in a fortnight. We know that he sent a copy to Pinker on 21 November and that he heard of Methuen's rejection of the typescript by 20 December.[19]

---

[17]See Appendix for a discussion of the textual evidence on which the following generalizations are based.

[18]Lawrence to Pinker, in possession of Forster.

[19]Catherine Carswell's recollection that "during January [1917] he had recomposed the first part of *Women in Love*" is puzzling and probably erroneous (*The Savage Pilgrimage* [New

From "The Sisters" to *Women in Love*

Whatever the exact time span, however, the exertion was great and the revisions extensive. Indeed, the revisions grew so extensive that he asked Frieda to help him transcribe his interlinear revisions of one typescript into the duplicate.[20] There is no evidence that Frieda herself did any revising, although in two places she has added a sentence in both typescripts, and in another she has corrected Lawrence's German.[21] Furthermore, Frieda's hand appears in *both* duplicates because each is a "composite" duplicate. What seems to have happened is that Lawrence and Frieda did not gather the pages into complete type-

---

York: Harcourt, Brace & Co., 1932], p. 83). If interpreted to mean that Lawrence continued revising through Jan., it would imply that the Carswells and perhaps Pinker and Methuen read the unrevised version. Surely this is very unlikely, since Lawrence began revising immediately and would hardly have sent off the duplicates before finishing.

[20] It may be too that Lawrence was somewhat incapacitated after the arduous months of composing on the typewriter.

[21] Frieda added "There always is and always will be" to page 170, line 6 of both, but Lawrence excised the sentence when revising the final typescript. However, Frieda's revision of page 243, line 6 in both—"she had no reason for hating him" changed to "her hate was quite abstract"—was retained in the final draft and appears on ML, p. 225, line 15. On page 541 Lawrence had written "Ja, das war merkwurdig, das war famos—." Frieda changed the German exclamation to "Das war ausgezeichnet, das war famos," which was retained on p. 652 of the definitive, and remains the reading on ML, p. 463, line 11.

The Manuscripts

scripts until they had completed all the revision and transcription. Then, assuming that the duplicate pages were identical, they did not take the trouble to ensure that one duplicate typescript was all ribbon copy and the other all carbon copy. Consequently, the duplicate typescripts as we have them do not reflect accurately the method or sequence of revision and transcription.

This habit of haphazard compilation explains the fact that many pages contain transcriptions in both Lawrence's and Frieda's hand. The manner of revising and transcribing these pages may have been as follows. First, Lawrence worked on a portion of typescript, and Frieda copied his revisions into the duplicate portion. Then after a break Lawrence took up the duplicate portion with Frieda's transcriptions and continued the revisions in it; and Frieda, in turn, copied the revisions into the portion on which Lawrence had been previously working.

The rapidity with which the duplicates were prepared also accounts for the great number of discrepancies between the holograph interlinear revisions of one typescript and the transcriptions of those revisions in the duplicate. Taken together, the Texas and Toronto duplicates contain at least 78 pages on which there are mistranscriptions, omissions, or incorrect erasures. These apparent mistakes were made by both Frieda and Lawrence while copying Lawrence's revisions. Since both Lawrence and

Frieda worked on many of the pages alternately, it is sometimes difficult to tell who made a particular mistake. Therefore it is possible that in several cases where an apparent mistake comes in the midst of Lawrence's copying the change may have been intended. As a rule, however, the changes are obviously inadvertent.

Textual evidence proves conclusively that Lawrence sent the Toronto duplicate typescript to Pinker to be copied and that Pinker used it as the exemplar for the final typescript, or draft. In every case a further revision or correction by Lawrence in the Toronto duplicate, not present in the Texas one, is reproduced in the final typescript.

Furthermore, Lawrence extensively revised the subsequent final draft, crossing out or retyping as many as fifteen pages at a stretch. This thoroughgoing revision eliminated a good many of the mistakes which had been reproduced. In some cases they were eliminated because they occurred in a passage which Lawrence wholly revised or replaced. In other cases Lawrence recorrected the reading, either by restoring the revision that had been mistranscribed or omitted, or by inserting a new revision very close in spirit to the original.[22] Consequently, in the final draft there are less than 40 pages on which tran-

---

[22]Lawrence revised "night" to "universe" on p. 223, line 27 of the Texas duplicate, but failed to transcribe the revision into the Toronto. Subsequently, he revised "night" to "universe" once again in the final typescript.

The Manuscripts

scriptional irregularities carried over from the Toronto duplicate remain.[23]

On 21 November 1916 Lawrence forwarded one typescript to Pinker and the other to the Carswells, asking them to "make any corrections necessary" but warning them: "Don't let anybody else read it."[24] From several marginal comments signed with the initials "D. C." (Donald Carswell), it is evident that the Carswells read what is now the Toronto duplicate. For example, where Lawrence had alluded to "Eleanor Duse, panting with her lovers after the theatre," a reader, presumably Carswell, who was a barrister, has written "this is a grave libel."[25] Lawrence finally corrected the passage in the proof sheets to read "the great Rachel . . .," after he had been warned again by Martin Secker that the reference might be "actionable."[26]

He ran into immediate trouble. Despite his injunctions of secrecy, Lady Ottoline Morrell had heard of the novel's contents: "I heard from Ottoline this morning, saying she hears she is the villainess of

---

[23] A comprehensive list of these substantive variants can be found in my article "A Problem of Textual Transmission in the Typescripts of *Women in Love*," *The Library*, 29, (1974), 197–205.

[24] Harry T. Moore, *Intelligent Heart*, rev. ed. (Harmondsworth: Penguin, 1960), p. 278.

[25] Toronto typescript, p. 612.

[26] For Secker's opinion see *Letters from a Publisher*, p. 11; for Lawrence's reply see *Letters from Lawrence to Secker*, p. 38.

From "The Sisters" to *Women in Love*

the new book . . . —so I have offered to send her the MS—So don't send it to Pinker till I let you know" (*CL*, p. 488, 27 Nov. 1916). Once the secret had been divulged, Lawrence acceded to the requests of friends and acquaintances—including Barbara Low, Esther Andrewes, and Mrs. Hilda Aldington—to read the typescript. Worse news followed. By 20 December 1916 he knew that "Methuen, having had the MS., agrees to cancel the agreement" (*CL*, p. 494). So there can be no doubt that the Texas duplicate was circulating among publishers and the Toronto among friends.[27]

With this chronology of composition and revision in mind, it is possible to interpret Lawrence's puzzling claim on 21 July 1916 that he was working on "the fourth and the final draft" of the novel (*CL*,

---

[27]Further evidence suggesting that Lady Ottoline and the other friends read the Toronto duplicate is supplied by her memoirs, where she describes her shock at finding herself transmogrified into Hermione Roddice: "Lawrence had mentioned in a letter . . . that he was writing about me in his new novel, but I didn't trouble myself about it until the MS arrived. I read it and found myself going pale with horror, for nothing could have been more vile and obviously spiteful and contemptuous than the portrait of me that I found there. . . . The only assuagement to the shock was that all the worst parts were written in Frieda's handwriting" (*Ottoline at Garsington*, ed. Robert Gathorne-Hardy [London: Faber & Faber, 1974], p. 128). Her suspicion of Frieda's malice was probably based on the prominence of Frieda's hand in the revisions of the Toronto duplicate.

The Manuscripts

p. 469). Lawrence, as we shall see, made four drafts of *Women in Love* when he began again on "The Sisters" in 1916 — two in holograph and two in typescript. So far we have examined the two holograph drafts, which survive only in fragments, and the duplicate typescripts, or penultimate draft. By his own count, however, Lawrence made *five* drafts.[28] The discrepancy arises because he evidently considered the fragments of his earlier work on "The Sisters" in 1913–14, which he had kept by him, to be one "draft." The two surviving fragments of that early material, "Sisters I" and "Sisters II," refer to characters whom Lawrence did not use in *The Rainbow:* Mrs. Crich, Gerald, Loerke, and Birkin. We have seen that as the scope of *The Rainbow* widened, draft by draft, Lawrence found that he would not be able to treat the later development of Ursula's story in one novel. In "The Wedding Ring," the penultimate version of *The Rainbow*, he may have compressed the story of Ursula (or "Ella," as she was called then) and Birkin into a mere 80 pages. When the rapidly expanding final version threatened to overflow the bounds of a one-volume novel, Lawrence decided to treat the story of Ursula and Birkin as a second novel. It is likely, then, that the 80 pages

---

[28] At the time he wrote to Pinker about the "fourth and final draft," Lawrence was typing the "original" typescripts, which were followed by a "definitive" typescript. Hence, by Lawrence's count, he made five drafts.

From "The Sisters" to *Women in Love*

from "The Wedding Ring" were part of the surviving material that Lawrence had at hand when he began the sequel to *The Rainbow*. And he may have considered them a "first draft" of *Women in Love*.

The "second draft" would then be the effort from which the two rejected chapters survive, entitled by George Ford "Prologue" and "The Wedding." Although the size of the draft cannot be judged with any certainty, it is unlikely that it was very long, because Lawrence had written another full holograph draft by June. Since he did not include the substance of "The Prologue" in any subsequent draft, he may have considered this false start as the second draft.

Putting aside these trial chapters, he wrote out a full draft in holograph between April and June 1916 — the third draft of the novel. Therefore the composition on the typewriter from July through October, incorporating "a lot of the original draft that I couldn't have bettered" (*CL*, p. 482), was "the fourth and the final draft." Indeed, four of the ten exercise books in which Lawrence wrote the last one-third of the final draft, after abandoning typing, show signs of having been part of the third draft. The title "The Sisters" and alternative pagination on four of the books are crossed out. In their place Lawrence has put "Women in Love" and started the page numbering with "1," even though the holograph exercise books continue from page 368 of the subsequent, or penultimate, draft. The change of ti-

The Manuscripts

tle is significant because Lawrence called the third draft "The Sisters" and even typed that title at the top of the first page of the fourth draft. It was not until he had typed more than half of the fourth draft that he considered "The Latter Days" and finally "Women in Love," which he decided to keep on 7 November 1916 (*CL*, p. 482). There are also patches of heavy revision in the exercise books. Therefore, it may be that Lawrence revised the last part of the third draft as the final one-third of the fourth draft, instead of starting the remainder of the fourth draft from scratch. Such seems to have been the sequence of the four drafts.

Furthermore, the manuscript exercise books clarify an often misinterpreted statement by Lawrence that he had finished "all but the last chapter, which, being a sort of epilogue, I want to write later —when I get the typescript back from you" (*CL*, p. 480, 31 Oct. 1916). This has usually been taken to mean that Lawrence delayed writing "Exeunt."[29] Yet the exercise books contain the substance of "Exeunt," and the penultimate draft does not show any break in textual continuity. But the tenth and last exercise book does contain one page of a further chapter that would truly have been an epilogue. This page reads:

A year afterwards, Ursula in Italy received a letter from Gudrun in Frankfurt am Main. Since the death of Gerald

---

[29]See, for example, Davis, pp. 52–53.

From "The Sisters" to *Women in Love*

in the Tyrol, when Gudrun had gone away, ostensibly to England, Ursula had had no news of her sister.

"I met a German artist who knew you," Gudrun said "and he gave me your address. I was silent for so long because there was nothing I could say.

"I have got a son—he is six months old now. His hair is like the sun shining on the sea, and he has his father's limbs and body. I am still Frau Crich—what actually happened is so much better, to account for one's position, than a lie would be. The boy is called Ferdinand Gerald Crich.

"As for the past—I lived for some months with Loerke, as a friend. Now I am staying

It is impossible to say how much of the epilogue Lawrence wrote before he abandoned it. Gudrun's pregnancy is reminiscent of the material of "Sisters I," although the latter fragment does not hint at the tragic consequences of Gudrun's relationship with Gerald.

CHAPTER 6

The Final Draft, *Women in Love*

Having labored strenuously at the novel for eight months, to the point of making himself ill, Lawrence rested in the months following the completion of the penultimate draft: "This is a kind of interval in my life, like a sleep. One only wanders through the dim short days, and reads, and cooks, and looks across at the sea. I feel as if I also were hibernating" (*CL*, p. 486). For Lawrence, "hibernating" meant reading American literature, about which he was already meditating "a set of essays or lectures," and writing short stories and the philosophical essays called *The Reality of Peace*.[1] All this hibernating activity is the more remarkable given Lawrence's avowed pessimism about creating art concerned with humans, particularly Englishmen. During January 1917 he tried, with the help of Mountsier and Pinker, to get exit visas for America: "I find I am unable to write for England any more — the response has gone quite dead and dumb. A certain hope re-

---

[1] He wrote "The Horse Dealer's Daughter" by 26 Jan. 1917 and "Samson and Delilah" before Mar.

From "The Sisters" to *Women in Love*

sides in my heart, quite hot, and I can go on. But it is not England. It seems to me it is America" (*CL*, p. 498).[2] Yet within two months, denied exit permission, he was denouncing and exhorting the English in *The Reality of Peace*. More serious for his art than this mood of "Damn Humanity" (*CL*, p. 491), was his apparent boredom with fiction: "There is no writing and publishing news. Philosophy interests me most now — not novels or stories. I find people ultimately boring: and you can't have fiction without people. So fiction does not, at the bottom, interest me any more. I am weary of humanity and human things. One is happy in the thoughts only that transcend humanity." (*CL*, p. 514, 23 May 1917). Behind his disillusionment lay the hostile response of publishers and public to the creative efforts of four years.[3] After such somber words, it is scarcely believable to find him undertaking yet another full-scale reconsideration and revision of *Women in Love*.

While the penultimate draft was still circulating among publishers and friends, S. S. Koteliansky suggested publishing a Russian translation of the novel in Russia.[4] According to Catherine Carswell, Kot

---

[2] He was refused visa endorsement by 12 Feb. (*CL*, p. 500).

[3] The penultimate draft of *Women in Love* was rejected by Methuen (Dec. 1916) and Duckworth (Jan. 1917). Fisher-Unwin also rejected a Ms., probably the final draft, in Dec. 1917.

[4] See Zytaruk, ed., *Quest for Rananim*, p. 104 (18 Dec. 1916).

The Final Draft

made the suggestion as a way of lending Lawrence money without injuring his pride.[5] Lawrence welcomed the idea and thought it a good opportunity to have several duplicates made into the bargain: "Don't you think it would be well to have a duplicate, or even two duplicate copies made at the same time? It is rather doubtful when the novel will be printed. And I have no written MS., because I recomposed all the first part on the typewriter. So I should be very glad if you would make for me a fair typed copy, at the same time the one is being made for Koteliansky, for Russia."[6] How many copies Pinker actually made is a matter of conjecture since only one survives; but Lawrence implies in a letter written three years later that Pinker prepared four copies.[7] Whatever the total figure, at least two copies were made, which Lawrence acknowledged in letters of 28 March and 1 April.[8] This means that Lawrence could not have contemplated revision until 1917, notwithstanding the speculations of Delav-

---

[5] Carswell, p. 80.

[6] Lawrence to Pinker, 20 Jan. 1917, in possession of Forster.

[7] Justifying his conduct to Huebsch, Lawrence says that he told Pinker to send one of the "3 copies" he had (*CL*, p. 618). Lawrence had kept the fourth copy, which he considered the "final Ms." because it contained all the revisions. Only this final manuscript, the unique copy, survives.

[8] Lawrence to Pinker, 28 Mar. 1917, in possession of Forster; Lawrence to Koteliansky, 1 Apr. 1917, in Zytaruk, ed., *Quest for Rananim,* pp. 112–13,

enay and Ford that November to January are the latest possible dates for "any substantial modification" of the text.[9]

The final typescript was prepared, as we have seen, from the Toronto duplicate of the penultimate draft. There is heavy interlinear revision throughout, solely in Lawrence's hand. In quantity the revisions of the final draft far surpass those of the penultimate; frequently the revisions became so extensive that Lawrence retyped or inserted long portions. He made a prodigious effort, reworking certain stretches at least twice. Consequently, the dating of these revisions is a delicate task that must be approached with the aid of the letters, especially several that have not been previously published.

The manuscript seems to have been revised at two quite separate times. The first period of revision was by far the most creative. The secondary revisions, which seem to comprise a distinct group by themselves, are not only far less numerous but are intended to refine or clarify the previous phase.[10] These so-called secondary revisions are made in reddish-brown ink, quite distinct from the blue used for the major phase, in a small, neat hand wherever space was available. The reddish-brown ink also appears on the extra title sheet that Lawrence probably added to the manuscript when he sent it to

[9]Ford, "Prologue," p. 99.

[10]Almost all of the 1919 revisions further refine the Birkinian notion of marriage, both heterosexual and homosexual.

The Final Draft

Thomas Seltzer in New York in 1919—hence the specification of country in the address: "Hermitage, nr. Newbury Berks., England."[11]

Lawrence's interest in the long-dormant manuscript had been aroused in the summer of 1919 by an overture from Thomas Seltzer, the American publisher who was to become an enthusiastic exponent of Lawrence's work until bankruptcy ended his short-lived publishing career. Lawrence responded on 7 September 1919, from Hermitage:

> I had your cablegram—at least as enclosed. I was away, so there is some delay. I wanted moreover to go through the MS. of the novel once more. — I consider this the best of my books. — Please be careful with the MS., as it is the most complete one: — I am forwarding it to you by the next mail.
>
> Meanwhile Martin Secker writes that he would like to publish the book next spring, under its old title "The Sisters." He has another copy. — I would like the book to come first in America. I shall never forgive England "The Rainbow." — If you wished to publish this novel, would you like me to write a short Fore-word? — And which title do you prefer, "Women in Love," or "The Sisters."[12]

The foreword is dated 12 September 1919. By 30 September he mailed the manuscript to Seltzer (*CL*, p. 596). We can thus be reasonably sure that Lawrence took the opportunity in late August and early

---

[11] I am indebted for this suggestion to Professor Pierre Vitoux of the University of Montpellier.

[12] Lacy, ed., *Letters to Thomas and Adele Seltzer*, p. 3.

From "The Sisters" to *Women in Love*

September to make the secondary revisions.

The earlier and major phase of revision cannot be dated quite so precisely, although it can be confined to a period of eight months, from May to December 1917. Pinker had not prepared the final typescript until 1 April 1917. From January through May 1917 Lawrence repeatedly expressed his lack of interest in fiction and said he was not working on the novel. In May, however, he was excited by Cecil Palmer's show of interest in the novel.[13] On 25 June he directed Pinker to act, and on 9 July he expressed the intention of sending Palmer his own copy.[14] By 27 July, moreover, he asked Waldo Frank to "tell Huebsch [the American publisher], if he gets the MS. of the new novel, *Women in Love,* that this MS. needs correcting from the English copy, and needs a tiny foreword, which this other has" (*CL*, p. 520). The implication of "correcting" is surely that Lawrence had made some revisions in his own copy of the final typescript, spurred to renewed activity by the professions of interest by Palmer and Huebsch. The "tiny foreword" he refers to was apparently superseded by the "short Fore-word" he wrote in September 1919.

Nothing came of these schemes: Pinker never

---

[13] Lawrence to Ernest Collings, 31 May 1917, Humanities Research Library.

[14] Lawrence to Collings, 9 July 1917, Humanities Research Library.

The Final Draft

forwarded Huebsch a copy; and Cecil Palmer, after returning the typescript on 27 August, let the matter drop.[15] But Lawrence was not completely cast down by this rebuff. Indeed, there are echoes in the letters of phrases that occur in the revisions, and that *might* indicate he had already revised the novel or was in the process of doing so.[16] In November, having been evicted from Cornwall, he lived in London, where he claimed "I don't do any work—none at all—only read and see people" (*CL*, p. 530). Nevertheless, Campbell raised his hopes about publishing the novel with Maunsel in Dublin, and Lawrence wrote to J. M. Hone about the possibility (*CL*, p. 532). Hone was more taken with the philosophical treatise "At the Gates," but failed to place either the philosophy or the novel.

Lawrence next mentioned the novel in February 1918, but then in a tone that showed he was no

---

[15]Lawrence to Palmer, 27 Aug. 1917, Southern Illinois University Library, Carbondale. Lawrence thanks Palmer for returning the typescript.

[16]Lawrence's allusions in letters to a human-less world and the "star-singleness of paradisal souls" bear similarities to revisions of several chapters in the novel, specifically, "An Island," "Mino," and "Excurse." See letters to Waldo Frank of 15 Sept. 1917 (*CL*, pp. 524–25) and to S. S. Koteliansky of 23 Sept. 1917 (*CL*, p. 525). In the last he writes: "Henceforth I deal in single, sheer beings—nothing human, only the star-singleness of paradisal souls. This is the latest sort of swank: also true."

From "The Sisters" to *Women in Love*

longer vitally interested in publishing schemes, only weary: "The full story of the novel is that Beaumont does not want his name to come in at all, as it is not too good a name in the purity ears already. . . . It depends a good deal what Antoine B. [Bibesco] would think fit to fob out. If he would help a good deal with the initial cost, very nice of him. If not, this thing can wait. . . . Don't do anything you don't want to do—it isn't worth it."[17] And by then he had started the desultory composition of *Aaron's Rod*, which, together with the American essays, poems, short stories, and a book of history, absorbed his energies until summer 1919.[18] In short, between October 1917 and summer 1919 Lawrence had neither the occasion nor the time to do the sort of wholesale revision noticeable in the final draft. The fact that the five excisions and replacements, both holograph and typed, are on the same brand and size of paper further suggests that the revisions were done at the same time, in a burst of creativity. Therefore we may take Lawrence at his word in the 1919 preface when he says that the final draft was "altogether re-written and finished in Cornwall in

---

[17]Lawrence to Cynthia Asquith, 28(?) Feb. 1918, Humanities Research Library. See also *CL*, p. 548: "If I can publish, I shall publish. But ten to one I can't, and I don't care a straw either way."

[18]Moreover, Lawrence was very ill with influenza in early 1919.

The Final Draft

1917." We may conclude with considerable confidence that he had finished the major phase of revision before he left Cornwall in October 1917, having worked again on the final draft between May and October.

CHAPTER 7

The Proofs: Censorship and Revision

After misunderstanding, accusations of duplicity, and hurried letters, Thomas Seltzer finally published the first edition of *Women in Love* in New York in 1920. Publication had been delayed over three years by a combination of Lawrence's notoriety following the cause célèbre of *The Rainbow*, threats of libel suits by Lady Ottoline Morrell and others, and Pinker's failure to promote the book. Huebsch complained belatedly that Pinker had never offered the novel to him. Lawrence tried ineffectually to withdraw the manuscript from Seltzer for Huebsch, but Seltzer refused to abort his edition.

One result of transatlantic publication was that Lawrence probably did not read the proofs of Seltzer's edition in time to have his corrections incorporated in the first edition. In his diary for 2 August 1920 Lawrence noted both receipt of Seltzer's galleys and his departure from Sicily.[1] He wandered in Italy

[1] E. W. Tedlock, Jr., *The Frieda Lawrence Collection of D. H. Lawrence Manuscripts* (Albuquerque: Univ. of New Mexico Press, 1948), p. 91; Harry T. Moore, *Poste Restante* (Berkeley: Univ. of California Press, 1956), pp. 60–61.

The Proofs

until 20 October. In the surviving correspondence he does not mention the proofs again until his return on 7 November, when it appears that he has just read them: "Thank you for all the proofs of *Women in Love*. I went through them. There are only very slight incorrections. I am looking forward to your volume: it comes out immediately, Mountsier [American agent] says."[2] Seltzer's private edition was published on 9 November in New York.

Whatever the extent of Lawrence's involvement with the Seltzer proofs, he could not have checked their accuracy against the manuscript, which Seltzer retained. Seltzer forwarded this manuscript directly to Secker, who rushed batches of proof of his English edition to Lawrence in Italy.[3] Consequently, Lawrence did not compare *either* set of proofs with the manuscript.

This point is worth mentioning because it should influence the choice of a copy text for a critical edition of *Women in Love*. David Farmer, who is preparing such an edition, has written that "it is proper to consider one of the American editions [i.e., Seltzer's] as copy text."[4] He does not discuss the

---

[2] Lacy, ed., *Letters to Thomas and Adele Seltzer*, p. 15.

[3] Lawrence discussed these proof corrections at length. See *Letters from Lawrence to Secker*, pp. 31, 34, 35.

[4] David Farmer, "*Women in Love*: A Textual History and Premise for a Critical Edition," in *Editing British and American Literature, 1880–1920*, ed. Eric Domville (New York: Garland Publishing Co., 1976), p. 91.

issue of proofreading or his reasons for preferring Seltzer's first edition to the extant manuscript from which it was prepared. As far as the letters permit one to judge, the manuscript has the greater authority as copy text.

The textual history of the first English edition, published by Martin Secker in 1921, is very complicated — and largely belongs to the history of the printed text, which is not our concern. The page proofs of the Secker edition, preserved in the Texas collection, are corrected by Lawrence in ink. In comparison to the substantial and pervasive revision of *The Rainbow* proofs, however, the corrections of *Women in Love* are slight and infrequent. Although a critic finds comparatively little to remark on, an editor finds a Chinese puzzle of intentions to solve. Martin Secker suggested many changes, demanded others, and made still others without Lawrence's knowledge or permission. At the same time Lawrence made a few voluntary, aesthetically motivated changes. For instance, the Seltzer first edition did not contain chapter headings, but Lawrence wrote these into the contents page of the Secker proofs at Martin Secker's request.[5] Then Secker suggested that Lawrence remove "the references [in chapter 7] to the unconventional manner in which the occupants of [Halliday's] flat used to sit about in the

---

[5]*Letters from a Publisher*, p. 6.

morning"[6] — that is, naked. Lawrence dutifully robed the men: Birkin appears not "in a state of nudity" but "in white pyjamas";[7] and Gerald stares at the "group of men," not the "group of naked men."[8] Several months later Secker further suggested the diminution of sexually explicit phrases, like that describing the sleeping arrangements of Loerke and his male companion, Leitner, who "lived together in the last degree of intimacy" in the proofs (and Seltzer edition). The change has them noncommittally "sharing the same bedroom."[9] While acceding to Secker's requests, Lawrence initiated a few changes. In the final draft version of chapter 3, for example, when Ursula is first attracted by Birkin's "curious hidden richness . . . the powerful beauty of life itself," she has an unexpected vision of "the magic of his thighs." Lawrence removed the reference from the Secker page proofs,

---

[6]This portion of the letter, omitted in *Letters from a Publisher*, was deciphered in the letterbooks by Farmer, to whose article I am indebted for many examples. Farmer and I had been independently studying the textual changes for several years before we became aware of each other's work. Our interests overlap but remain largely independent. Whereas he is interested primarily in the history of the printed text, I am interested in the history of the manuscripts.

[7]Secker proof, p. 80; ML, p. 87; V, p. 71.
[8]Secker proof, p. 81; ML, p. 88; V, p. 71.
[9]Secker proof, p. 445; ML, p. 481; V, p. 412.

From "The Sisters" to *Women in Love*

perhaps because he recognized that he had forced the issue: "It was in the curves of his brows and his chin, rich, fine, exquisite curves, the powerful beauty of life itself [, something like laughter, invisible and satisfying. Also the magic of his thighs had fascinated her: the inner slopes of his thighs]. She could not say what it was."[10] Whereas Ursula can react plausibly to the beauty of his face, she cannot to that of his thighs hidden in a shapeless suit. The eventual praise of Birkin's thighs and loins in "Excurse" gains whatever credibility it possesses from such naturalistic details as Ursula observing him crouching by the pond ("An Island") and Gudrun observing Gerald floundering in and out of a boat in "Water-Party." Lawrence had anticipated his art.

The most substantial single alteration in the text, however, was probably made by Secker without Lawrence's knowledge. It obscures the most explicit passage concerning homosexuality, in which Birkin all but proposes a sexual aspect to *Blutbrüderschaft* that would place a male homosexual marriage on a basis of equality with heterosexual marriage. The following passage, which appears in both the page proofs and the Seltzer edition, was excised from the Secker:

Gerald moved uneasily. "You know I can't feel that," said he. "Surely there can never be anything as strong

[10]Secker proof, p. 46; ML, pp. 48–9; V, p. 38.

The Proofs

between man and man as sex love is between man and woman. Nature doesn't provide the basis."

"Well, of course, I think she does. And I don't think we shall ever be happy till we establish ourselves on this basis. You've got to get rid of the *exclusiveness* of married love. And you've got to admit the unadmitted love of man for man. It makes for a greater freedom for everybody, a greater power of individuality both in men and women."[11]

Everything we know of Lawrence's intentions in revising the friendship of Gerald and Birkin suggests that he would not have countenanced this crucial deletion. It was a passage, after all, that he had probably inserted as late as September 1919 in a last effort to clarify the Birkinian notion of a mystic marriage between men. One concludes that Secker, who had already paid a libel claimant, took the liberty of acting in what he considered to be the author's and his own best interests.

Although we are not concerned to trace the vicissitudes of the printed text, we should note that the second and third printings of the Secker first edition contain many alterations of the Halliday-Pussum-Pompadour scenes occasioned by Philip Heseltine's threats of a libel suit. Frightened by Heseltine,

---

[11]Secker proof, p. 372; ML, p. 403; V, p. 345. That is, the passage appears in Seltzer's edition and the Secker proofcopy, but not in the Secker first edition. See Farmer, pp. 89-90.

From "The Sisters" to *Women in Love*

Secker sent snippets of the already corrected page proofs to Italy, requesting Lawrence to alter such details as the physical description of Halliday and Pussum, Pussum's name, and the provenience of the fetish statue (from Africa to the West Indies) so as to avoid a libel action.[12] Lawrence complied and asked Secker to go through the rest of the proofs to alter the other references in the subplot. But Secker neglected to do so. Eventually Heseltine was satisfied with the sum of sixty pounds and ten shillings. These hurried alterations, done incompletely under pressure, account for many of the inconsistencies in current editions.[13]

---

[12]Lawrence to Secker, 8 Oct. 1921: "I enclose the altered pages. The Pussum I have made a blue-eyed fair-haired little thing. Halliday black and swarthy: the manservant an Arab: the flat a house in St. John's Wood. For this last item, *please correct in a previous chapter*. Please go through it all carefully, to see there are no discrepancies.

"I think it is all perfect nonsense—as if there weren't dozens of little Pussums about Chelsea, and dozens of Hallidays anywhere. But I do it since you wish it" (*Letters from Lawrence to Secker*, p. 44).

[13]A pioneering but less complete treatment of the text than Farmer's can be found in Eldon S. Branda, "Textual Change in *Women in Love*," *Texas Studies in Literature and Language*, 6 (1964), 306–31.

CHAPTER 8

Techniques of Revision in the Manuscripts

Having reconstructed the sequence of the drafts and the accidents of publication, we may sample the artistry of composition. For the manuscripts offer a fascinating look into the novelist's workshop that should dispel erroneous speculation about Lawrence's methods. Emile Delavenay, one of Lawrence's biographers, has asserted that Lawrence

> conceived the main outline of events, and the treatment of character, in the double novel *The Rainbow* and *Women in Love* before the war, over a period which extends from December 1912 to the summer of 1914; and . . . the bulk of the two novels was written before the outbreak of war. Of course details were added to *The Rainbow*, and even whole chapters and incidents to *Women in Love*, in the course of the final re-writing in 1915 and 1916 respectively, but both theme and method were determined by 1914.[1]

Delavenay gives no reason for disregarding Lawrence's clear testimony to the contrary: "This novel

---

[1]Emile Delavenay, *TLS*, p. 12.

From "The Sisters" to *Women in Love*

was written in its first form in the Tyrol, in 1913. It was altogether re-written and finished in Cornwall in 1917. So that it is a novel which took its final shape in the midst of the period of war, though it does not concern the war itself."[2] "Altogether re-written" is not an exaggeration, as anyone who consults the manuscripts will see. Let us recall a few of the facts which Delavenay overlooks. Lawrence did not create the Tom / Lydia generation until he began the final draft of *The Rainbow*. Although "Sisters I" did contain a version of parts of *Women in Love*, it presented all "The Sisters" material in 300 pages; so the treatment of the *Women in Love* story must have been brief. And the treatment of the relationship between Birkin and Ursula occupied a mere eighty pages in "The Wedding Ring." Therefore "the bulk of the two novels" was emphatically not written before the war.

To illustrate the creativity of Lawrence's techniques of revision, I shall choose one aspect of each of the three stories which interweave in the novel: those of Gerald Crich and Gudrun Brangwen, Rupert Birkin and Gerald, and Ursula Brangwen and Rupert.

Gerald Crich's most prominent characteristic, his Nordic appearance foreboding "the universal dissolution into whiteness and snow," was not men-

[2]ML, p. ix.

Techniques of Revision in the Manuscripts

tioned in the penultimate draft.[3] It emerged in the thoroughgoing revision of the final draft. In the penultimate, one can watch Lawrence gradually discovering his dramatic opportunity. The light though continual revision becomes heavy in the concluding Tyrolese chapters as though he were seeing at last the full possibilities of his materials. Having created the icy setting "in the heart of the mountains" for the climax of the penultimate draft, he was inspired in the final draft to add those aspects of character and theme that would seem to lead inevitably to the tragic death of Gerald and his world amid the "terrible waste of whiteness."[4] And these revisions inspired others as the novel grew into its final shape. Therefore we follow Lawrence's practice by starting at the end of the penultimate draft.

The inhuman and phenomenal aspect of the mountains suggested a complex of imagery in which to describe the powerful and ultimately self-destructive will that Gerald and Gudrun exert on each other and the world at large. Just as the dazzling white of the mountains reduces humans to "phenomena" and "snow-creatures," so Gerald treats his miners as "instruments . . . sporadic little unimportant phenomena," subduing man and beast with the same apparently indomitable "northern"

[3] ML, p. 290.
[4] ML, pp. 453, 455.

From "The Sisters" to *Women in Love*

will power. The resonance of this northern vocabulary for conveying the unnatural, nonorganic, and finally sterile abuse of the will that is characteristic of modern society struck Lawrence with such force that he rewrote scene after scene in the final draft to accentuate it. Virtually all the allusions to Gerald's northern presence are the result of that revision. Gudrun's first sight of him, for example, was revised as follows:

["*His* totem is the wolf," said Gudrun to herself, "a young, innocent, unconscious wolf." She wondered *how* innocent, and how far untameable. She would like to know. He looked a man of twenty eight or thirty, but young, unbroached.] <Gudrun lighted on him at once. There was something northern about him that magnetized her. In his clear northern flesh and his fair hair was a glisten like sunshine refracted through crystals of ice. And he looked so new, unbroached, pure as an arctic thing.>[5]

The way in which Lawrence harmonized the northern vocabulary in revision with the mechanical and life-denying nature of the will, giving a premonition of the end of such willfulness, is clear in the two scenes where Gerald subdues the mare and the rabbit (chapters 9 and 18, respectively):

[An ugly] <A sharpened> look came on Gerald's face. He bit himself down on the mare [with determination]

[5]Final draft, p. 14.

Techniques of Revision in the Manuscripts

<like a keen edge biting home> . . . Both man and horse were sweating with violence. <Yet he seemed calm as a ray of cold sunshine.>[6]

Then a sudden [deep, congenital anger] <sharp, white-edged wrath> came up in him . . . His face was [smiling with anger] <gleaming with a smile> . . . He looked at her [in wonder, and subterranean fear.] <and the whitish, electric gleam in his face intensified.>[7]

It would be misleading, however, to imply that Lawrence discovered the northern vocabulary while writing the penultimate draft. The inspiration was, as usual with him, a sudden distillation of thought and practice. In the discarded "Prologue" opening of the second draft, Birkin is drawn to two classes of men with differing complexions. The first class comprises "white-skinned, keen-limbed men with eyes like blue-flashing ice and hair like crystals of winter sunshine, the northmen, inhuman as sharp-crying gulls, distinct like splinters of ice, like crystals, isolated, individual."[8] Although Lawrence had fashioned the vocabulary in "Prologue," he did not apply it specifically to "the fair, keen-eyed Englishman." Apparently he did not see how to make use of it until he had written the end of the penultimate draft. Then, having transformed the "hunter . . .

[6]Final draft, pp. 169–70.
[7]Final draft, p. 382.
[8]Ford, "Prologue," p. 109.

From "The Sisters" to *Women in Love*

traveller . . . soldier" of the "Prologue" into an industrial magnate, he could make him the symbol of the winter of our epoch. By cumulative revisions Lawrence shows Gerald progressing from his initially appealing aspect as an "unbroached, pure . . . arctic thing," through increasingly sinister outbursts of northern will power as the deus ex machina of industrial Beldover and as one of the "strange white wonderful demons of the north" in Birkin's meditations, to his apotheosis as the "supernatural force" who literally turns to ice in the Tyrol. One moment in the chapter "Continental" must suffice: "He felt strong as [a weapon of] <winter, his hands were> living metal . . . [He had her in his power] <He was superhumanly strong and unflawed, as if invested with supernatural force> . . . His heart went up like a flame <of ice>, he closed over her like steel."[9]

Our second example comes from the Gerald Crich / Rupert Birkin story line. Chapter 16, "Man to Man," represents the first climax of the theme of male friendship, as the strong but suppressed affection between the two men is openly discussed. The penultimate version presents such friendship as hopeless and "perhaps death" because it is merely the complement to "the hatred for woman." Birkin demands an absolute surrender, and Ursula is

[9] Final draft, p. 642.

equally absolute in her assertions of female superiority. If Birkin appears a male chauvinist, Ursula has a good deal of the overweening female, or Magna Mater, about her. Recoiling from the impasse, Birkin turns to the love for Gerald, which he considers merely a despairing consolation. He has no hope in the revivifying possibilities of male friendship; without woman there can be no new life. Since he has decided that neither female nor male friendship offers an alternative to the imminent experience of death, he responds to Gerald's passionate approach with "cold weariness":

"Yes," Birkin admitted. "I like you better than anybody else—any other *man*."

He put out his hand from the bed, and took Gerald's brown, sinewy hand in his own. Convulsively, Gerald clasped Birkin's hand in both his, and sat with lips parted, breathing short and fast, his eyes set. Birkin looked at him, with unchanging eyes. He felt a hot pang of love for him, and a deep pity, a deep sorrow. Then finally, a cold weariness.

"We'll stand by each other, Gerald," he said slowly.

Gerald's face changed swiftly, he looked aside . . . he so much wanted the other man to take him in his arms and hold him close in peace and love. Yet it was so impossible.

"A Blutbrüderschaft," said Birkin, wearily, reassuring, as if to comfort the other.[10]

[10] Penultimate draft, p. 252.

From "The Sisters" to *Women in Love*

That is the only mention of *Blutbrüderschaft* in the penultimate draft. But the feeling of impossibility counters the physical immediacy of the moment, so that Birkin's offer carries no conviction. The friendship of Birkin and Gerald, like that of Birkin and Ursula, seems to have ended in frustration and unfulfilment.

Revising the final version, Lawrence grasped the full potential in what had appeared to be the impossible love of man for man, at least partly because he had also reconsidered the development of the Birkin / Ursula story. Birkin now sees with sudden clarity the need for an equally creative love between men, amplifying the solitary mention of *Blutbrüderschaft* into the keynote of his conversations with Gerald. However, his manner of advancing the idea is not dogmatic but dramatic. He looks "at Gerald with clear, happy eyes of discovery," but he must search for the right words to express the love he has been denying all along:

> "We will swear to each other, one day, shall we?" pleaded Birkin. "We will swear to stand by each other—be true to each other—ultimately—infallibly—given to each other, organically—without possibility of taking back."
>
> Birkin sought hard to express himself.[11]

The revision focuses on the urgency and sincerity of Birkin's words rather than their programmatic con-

---

[11]Final draft, p. 330a.

Techniques of Revision in the Manuscripts

Page 330 of the final draft of *Women in Love*. (Courtesy of the Humanities Research Library, University of Texas at Austin.)

From "The Sisters" to *Women in Love*

> 331.
> He lay in the bed, whilst his friend sat beside him, lost in brooding and wondering. Each man was gone in his own thoughts.
>
> "You know how the old German knights used to swear a Blutbrüderschaft," he said to Gerald, with quite a new happy activity in his eyes.
>
> "Make a little wound in their arms, and rub the each others blood into the cut?", said Gerald.
>
> "Yes — and swear to be true to each other, of one blood, all their lives. — That is what we ought to do. No wounds, that is obsolete. — But we ought to swear to love each other, you and I, implicitly and perfectly, finally, without any possibility of going back on it."
>
> He looked at Gerald with clear, happy eyes of discovery. Gerald looked down at him, attracted, so deeply bondaged in fascinated attraction, that he was mistrustful, resenting the bondage, hating the attraction.
>
> "We will swear to each other, one day, shall we?" pleaded Birkin. "We will swear to stand by each other — be true to each other — ultimately — infallibly — given to each other, organically, — without possibility of taking back."
>
> Birkin sought hard to express himself. But Gerald hardly listened. His face shone with a certain luminous pleasure. He was pleased. But he kept his reserve. He held himself back.
>
> "Shall we swear to each other, one day?", said Birkin, putting out his hand towards Gerald.
>
> Gerald just touched the extended fine, living hand, as if withheld and afraid. "We'll leave it till I understand it better," he said, in a voice of excuse.
>
> Birkin watched him. A little sharp disappointment, perhaps a touch of contempt came into his heart.
>
> "Yes," he said, "you must tell me what you think, later. You know what I mean? not sloppy emotionalism. An impersonal union that leaves one free." — They lapsed both into silence. Birkin was looking at Gerald all the time. He seemed now to see, not the physical, animal man, which he usually saw in Gerald, and which usually he liked so much, but the man himself, complete, and as if fated, doomed, limited. This

Page 330a of the final draft of *Women in Love*. (Courtesy of the Humanities Research Library, University of Texas at Austin.)

Techniques of Revision in the Manuscripts

331

strange sense of fatality in Gerald, as if he were united to ~~not look at Birkin's dark, steadfast eyes any more, he turned~~ one form of existence, one knowledge, one activity, a sort of fatal ~~aside, panting slightly, because he so much wanted the other~~ half-ness, which to himself seemed wholeness, always overcame ~~man to take him in his arms and hold him close in peace and~~ Birkin after their moments of passionate approach, and used him ~~love. Yet it was so impossible.~~ was the insistence on the imitation with a sort of contempt, or boredom. A deliberately
"A ~~Blutbrüderschaft,~~" said Birkin, ~~softly,~~ reassuring, as which so bored Birkin in Gerald. Gerald could never fly away from ~~if to comfort the other~~ himself, in real indifferent gaiety. He had a clog, a sort of monomania.

~~And~~ There was silence for a time. Then Birkin said, in a
                                            contact
lighter tone, letting the stress of the ~~emotion~~ pass:

"Can't you get a good governess for Winifred? - somebody exceptional?"

"Hermione Roddice suggested we should ask Gudrun to teach her to draw and to model in clay. You know Winnie is astonishingly clever with that plasticine stuff. Hermione declares she is an artist." Gerald spoke in the usual uninitated, chatty
full of reminders   manner, as if nothing unusual had passed. But Birkin's manner was
"Really! I didn't know that. - Oh well then, if Gudrun would teach her, it would be perfect - couldn't be anything
                              better—   Somewhere
~~more perfect~~ - if Winifred is an artist. Because Gudrun is one. And every true artist is the salvation of every other."

"I thought they got on so badly, as a rule."
                                       for each other
"Perhaps. But only artists produce the world that is fit to live in. If you can arrange that for Winifred, it is perfect."

"But you think she wouldn't come?"

"I don't know. Gudrun is rather self-opinionated. She won't go cheap anywhere. Or if she does, she'll pretty soon take herself back. So whether she would condescend to do private

Page 331 of the final draft of *Women in Love*. (Courtesy of the Humanities Research Library, University of Texas at Austin.)

From "The Sisters" to *Women in Love*

tent. Birkin, we feel, has seized on the Teutonic *Blutbrüderschaft* in order to appeal to his "soldierly" friend, who considers him too "uncertain" in the man's world. Lawrence does not appear to be primarily interested in elaborating the no doubt anachronistic form of pledging friendship. What is important to him as an artist is the way in which the friends react to the notion—Birkin eagerly and perhaps too insistently, Gerald ambivalently. For Gerald is both deeply attracted and mistrustful: "Gerald looked down at him, attracted, so deeply bondaged in fascinated attraction, that he was mistrustful, resenting the bondage, hating the attraction. . . . He held himself back."[12] Inspired by the discovery of male comradeship as a viable possibility in human relations, Lawrence used it as the growing point for the remainder of the Birkin / Gerald story. Even such a brief example should cast doubt on the too common opinion, based largely on the "Prologue," that Lawrence muted or concealed the homosexual theme of the novel for prudential or psychological reasons. What the drafts show is Lawrence creating meaning, not disguising it.

Finally, we may study an example from the Birkin / Ursula story line. The characterization of Birkin presented special problems of artistic objectivity. For the banned author living in exile in Cornwall as the World War destroyed civilization, the

[12] Ibid.

Techniques of Revision in the Manuscripts

temptation to place jeremiads in Birkin's mouth was great. It was so great that Lawrence often succumbed in the early drafts of the novel. One of the achievements of the finished novel, however, is its cogent criticism of Birkin's deficiencies and the clear difference between his dramatic voice and that of Lawrence. The exploratory artist did not give free reign to the misanthropist or moral absolutist we hear in the letters and essays of the period.

Having learned to dramatize Birkin's dogmatic attitudes, largely through the critical opposition of Ursula, Lawrence could make the didactic content of Birkin's speeches suggestive rather than programmatic—qualifying but not discarding them altogether.

The three rewritings of Birkin's poetical speech on the "river of dissolution" in the chapter "Water-Party" show the complexity of Lawrence's strategy in revising the characterization of Birkin and, in the process, his strict subordination of literary influences to the dramatic context of the novel. In the first two versions, Lawrence awkwardly uses touchstone quotations from the Pre-Socratic philosophers to introduce a stump speech by Birkin recapitulating much of the argument of *The Crown* in a dogmatic manner that deserves the devastating ridicule leveled at it by the sisters:

["All is two, fire and water, as Anaximander or Herakleitos or somebody says," he replied. "The motion

From "The Sisters" to *Women in Love*

of the one is up, the other, down. I think that is more true, as philosophy of the physical world, than anything else. . . . That is the Flux of Corruption, to which some people belong almost altogether, people like Wagner and D'Annunzio, and all the people who go back to early myths and to anthropology — all those whose great motion is the return to the origins."]

<"Everything, both physical and spiritual is passing upwards or downwards, as Herakleitos or somebody says," he replied, "upwards into fire and downwards into water — that is true."

"Why is it true?", laughed Ursula.

"Because all activity is twofold, production and corruption. There is the great flux of corruption, flowing back and back and resolving down and reducing everything produced, flowing back until you reach the original universality. That is the flux of Corruption, to which some people belong almost altogether, all those whose great motion is the return to the origins. It has its blossoms just as fire has its blossoms. Swans and waterlilies and sea-born Aphrodite, they all belong to that stream. And it is the equal of production, because it is its opposite, therefore it is its equivalent."

"And what are you? Do you belong to the Flux of Corruption too?" laughed Ursula.

"Both. There are two fires, the slow cold fire of corruption, that returns to the origin, and the quick fire that consumes into the ultimate One, all the many things that there are now. But life is a resultant of these two — all life. The flame of the cold fire rushing germinating against the flame of the hot fire, suddenly a fusion takes place within the fiery regions, and that's a poppy — or you — or

Techniques of Revision in the Manuscripts

me—or a tiger. But when the hot flame darts and germinates in the cold stream of the fires of corruption, then within the flux of corruption is born a lotus flower, or a swan, or Hermione, or the nereids."

"How very lovely!" cried Gudrun. "So I shall know now, how to place people. They are either flux of corruption—"

"Mostly that," interrupted Birkin, with equanimity.

"Oh are they? . . . But *you* are the other. What is the other?"

"The fiery flame," he said, smiling.

"How beautiful! So the thing to do is to say to people, 'Are you Flux of Corruption, or Fiery Flame?' And then, of course, if they are Flux, you don't have anything to do with them."

"It depends," he said. "Flux is just as *good* as Flame. It all rests on what you want."

"Oh, does it? Then there's a new heart-searching now. It's not, do I love God as I ought, but do I lean to Flux or to Flame?"

"A much more pertinent question," he laughed. >[13]

As a result of Gudrun's mockery, Birkin looks merely foolish and his ideas ridiculous. In the final version, however, Lawrence was able to place Birkin's theo-

---

[13]Penultimate draft, pp. 209–211. On 5 Sept. 1916 Lawrence asked Dolly Radford: "Has Maitland got Burnet's *Early Greek Philosophers?* If he has, I should be glad if he would lend it me—I want to refer to it" (*CL*, pp. 473–74). Presumably he was composing the first version of "Water-Party" at the time.

From "The Sisters" to *Women in Love*

rizing as part of a character who is in many ways admirable.[14] Although he may be ridiculous in his manner of pronouncing absolute truths, he does have the vital instinct to search for an alternative to the deathliness of social and human relations. Therefore he must be subjected to irony but not wholly discredited. So Gudrun is not a party to the conversation in the final draft; Birkin and Ursula wrestle with their fate alone. But Ursula, as a more skeptical audience, probes the argument with pertinent questions and forces Birkin to temper his dogmatism. Under her prodding he admits that although "some people are pure flowers of dark corruption . . . there ought to be some roses, warm and flamy." The "flamy" recalls two previous occasions when Birkin admires Ursula's flamy, antagonistic personality—both of which were added contemporaneously with the revisions of "Water-Party." For example, in the chapter "Mino": "He stood smiling in frustration and amusement and irritation and admiration and love. She was so quick, and so lambent, like discernible fire, and so vindictive, and so rich in her dangerous flamy sensitiveness."[15] And Ursula's half-mocking suggestion that Birkin thinks all people *fleurs du mal* draws on the later mockery of his misguided rhetoric by Halliday's crowd in

---

[14] The final version, too long to quote, runs from ML, p. 195, line 30, to p. 197, line 18.

[15] Final draft, p. 239; ML, p. 171.

Techniques of Revision in the Manuscripts

"Gudrun in the Pompadour." Just as the Halliday scene mocks the worst excesses of *The Crown* without discrediting the sincerity or seriousness of the intellectual attempt, so the revisions of "Water-Party" qualify the portentousness but not the need for such speculation.

Ursula's skeptical presence, moreover, allows Lawrence to make the speech both more compelling and more adequate to the thematic life of the novel. The penultimate version had confused the issue of flux versus flame by having Birkin say: "It depends . . . Flux is just as *good* as Flame. It all depends on what you want." This riposte was unsatisfactory on two counts. First, it implied that neither flux nor flame is better than the other, except subjectively. Secondly, it neglected to mention history: Do flux and flame vary with the historical context? Can people choose with such complete freedom as Birkin implies when he says: "It all depends on what you want"? The final version goes some way toward meeting both objections. By choosing Heraclitus' dictum that "a dry soul is best," Lawrence points to the differences even within the process of corruption. The quotation has an appositeness to the novel lacking in the earlier forced borrowings from the Pre-Socratics, recalling Gerald's exultation in the water world of "Diver" and foreshadowing his imminent immersion later in the chapter. The revised conversation also takes history into account. Birkin's prediction that there will be "a new cycle of creation" after the end of this era continues the speculation, which grows more urgent as the novel progresses. Yet the increasingly dire vision is held in check by Ursula's opposition, and the historical prediction becomes a point of discussion to be tested by the course of the novel. By both criticizing and bolstering Birkin, Lawrence has made the chapter more suggestive and dramatic.

To trace the history of the composition of *Women in Love* is to marvel at Lawrence's energy, pertinacity, and inventiveness. Sick in body and spirit and faced with either indifference or open hostility from publishers and the reading public, he wrote and revised four full-length drafts of the novel. The eighty pages that may have remained from the discarded "The Wedding Ring" expanded, over three and a half years, into the superb novel we now read. In the place of the erroneous picture of Lawrence inserting "details" and "even whole chapters" into a text that had been finished in 1914, we must envisage Lawrence experimenting continuously and laboring unremittingly on a work that was altogether new. The history of the novel is a unique tribute to the creativity of the human spirit.

Appendix

A Problem of Transmission in the Typescripts of *Women in Love*

The duplicate typescripts that constitute the novel's third draft are composite in the sense of being a mixture of both ribbon copy and carbon copy. Moreover, they contain a number of transcriptional dissimilarities. Therefore, it might be said that, strictly speaking, neither of the typescripts is a duplicate in the full sense of the word. For clarity of reference, the so-called duplicates have been called simply the Texas and the Toronto typescripts.

A further difficulty in terminology is the fact that both duplicate typescripts have been called "original." This difficulty has arisen because the Texas collection calls the Texas duplicate original in the sense of being anterior in the lineage of composition to the final manuscript from which the proof sheets were made. Hence, if one followed the Texas system of classification, the Toronto duplicate would also be original. But the designation of both typescripts as original confuses the issue; for, as the following demonstrates, only the Toronto typescript was used to prepare the final manuscript. Therefore

Appendix

the Toronto typescript is the true original of the final.[1]

The following analyzes three pages chosen to represent the various kinds of textual evidence on which I have reconstructed the stages of revision and the order of the texts.

1. The letter *a* added to a line number refers to the autograph revision directly *above* the line. For example, 1.10a means the interlinear holograph revision above line 10.

2. Texas = the Texas typescript, Toronto = the Toronto typescript (i.e., original manuscripts). Final = the final typescript (i.e., final manuscript).

Page 1

Page 1 shows three stages of revision. In a first run through, Lawrence changed "have" to "do" in line 11a of both. In the second stage, revisions made in the Toronto were transcribed in the Texas (i.e., intermediate revisions of lines 10a, 16a, 17a, and 18a of Toronto are transcribed fair in Texas). Finally,

---

[1]For the purposes of a general study of the revisions, the differences between the Texas and Toronto typescripts are negligible; for minute textual study and a future restoration of the published text, however, they are important. See my article "A Problem of Textual Transmission in the Typescripts of *Women in Love*" for a list of the variants that found their way into the published text.

Appendix

Lawrence appears to have prepared the Toronto for Pinker to have typed, crossing out "all" in 1.9a. The "all," present in the Texas, does not appear in the final manuscript made from one of the duplicates. The deduction follows that the corresponding page of the final manuscript was made from this page of the Toronto typescript.

Page 2

Page 2 raises a typical problem of precedence. Following the usual light, preliminary revision in both, Lawrence appears to have worked on the Toronto at the top and on the Texas at the bottom. That is, intermediate revisions at the top of the Toronto page are transcribed fair in the Texas page, and vice versa for the bottom of the page. (e.g., At top of Toronto see line 7a, where "kind of" is crossed out and line 8a, where "fairly" is also crossed out. At bottom of Texas, see line 21a, where "marriage" becomes "match.")

Page 249

Page 249 introduces Frieda's role in the process of transcription. It also raises the questions whether her changes in transcription were intended or inadvertent and whether Lawrence overlooked or endorsed them. Finally, it provides evidence that the Toronto typescript became the exemplar for the final manuscript.

After the preliminary stage (see line 1a), it appears that Lawrence worked on the Texas and that Frieda transcribed into the Toronto. But Frieda miscopied in line 5a, writing "harm" instead of Lawrence's "hurt." This mistake or correction on Frieda's part would be of little importance were it not that the final manuscript and the published novel retain her reading. Whether Lawrence approved her correction or overlooked her mistake, it is clear that the corresponding page in the final manuscript was copied from the Toronto typescript, thus providing more evidence that the final manuscript followed the Toronto duplicate.

Conclusion

The perplexing alternation of copy in the duplicate typescripts is adventitious. There is no evidence that Freida revised; her role in the preparation of the typescripts was limited to transcription. All the evidence points toward the identification of the Toronto typescript as the chosen exemplar for the final manuscript.

Appendix

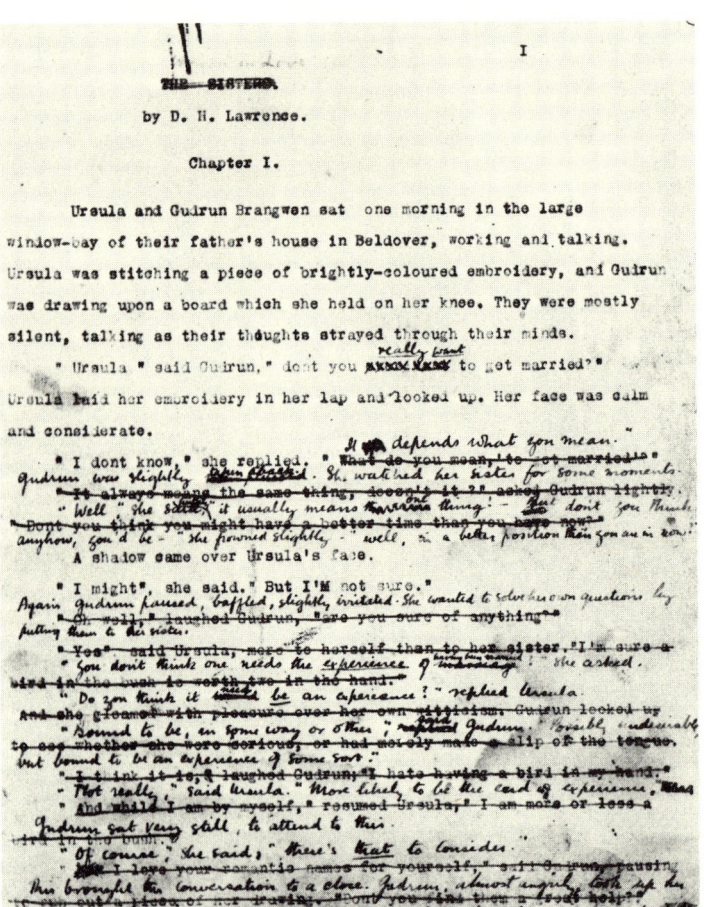

Page 1 of the Toronto typescript of *Women in Love*. (Courtesy of the Thomas Fisher Rare Book Library, University of Toronto.)

Appendix

<u>Women in Love</u>.
~~THE SISTERS.~~

by D. H. Lawrence.

Chapter I.

Ursula and Gudrun Brangwen sat one morning in the large window-bay of their father's house in Beldover, working and talking. Ursula was stitching a piece of brightly-coloured embroidery, and Gudrun was drawing upon a board which she held on her knee. They were mostly silent, talking as their thoughts strayed through their minds.

"Ursula," said Gudrun, "dont you really want to get married?" Ursula laid her embroidery in her lap and looked up. Her face was calm and considerate.

"I dont know," she replied. "It all depends what you mean." Gudrun was slightly taken aback. She watched her sister for some moments. "Well," she said, huffly, "it usually means one thing! — But dont you think, anyhow, you'd be — the fermed slightly, — "well, in a better position than you are in now?" A shadow came over Ursula's face.

"I might", she said. "But I'M not sure."
Again Gudrun paused, baffled, slightly irritated. She wanted to solve her own question by putting them to her sister.

"Feel," said Ursula, more to herself than to her sister. "I'm sure — you dont think one needs the experience of having been married?" she asked.
"Do you think it need be an experience?" replied Ursula.
"Bound to be, in one way or another," said Gudrun. "Possibly, undesirable, but bound to be an experience of some sort."

"Not really," retorted Ursula. "More likely to be the end of experience."
"And while I am by myself," resumed Ursula,

"Of course," she said, "there's that to consider."
his brought the conversation to a close. Gudrun, almost angrily, took up her rubber and began to rub out part of her drawing. Ursula stitched absorbedly.

Page 1 of the Texas typescript of *Women in Love*. (Courtesy of the Humanities Research Library, University of Texas at Austin.)

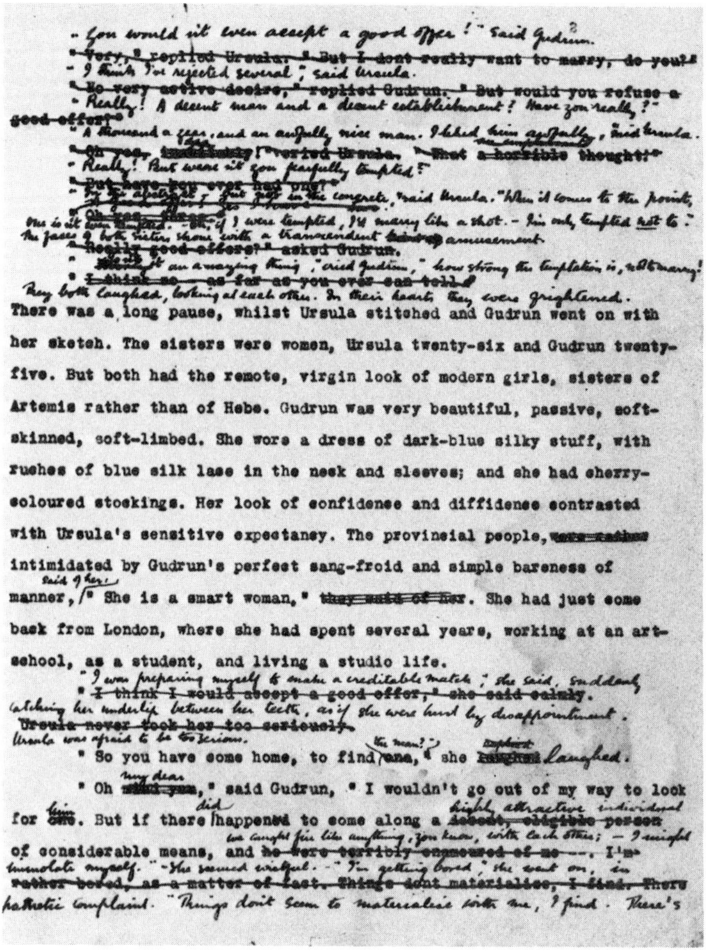

"You would not even accept a good offer!" said Gudrun.
~~"Very," replied Ursula. "But I dont really want to marry, do you?"~~
"I think I've rejected several," said Ursula.
~~"No very active desire," replied Gudrun. "But would you refuse a good offer?"~~
"Really! A decent man and a decent establishment! Have you really?"
"A thousand a year, and an awfully nice man. I liked him awfully," said Ursula.
"Really! But were not you fearfully tempted?"
"In the abstract, but not in the concrete," said Ursula. "When it comes to the point, I'm not even tempted. – Oh, if I were tempted, I'd marry like a shot. – I'm only tempted not to." The faces of both sisters shone with a transcendent amusement.
"Isn't it an amazing thing," cried Gudrun, "how strong the temptation is, not to marry!"
They both laughed, looking at each other. In their hearts they were frightened.

There was a long pause, whilst Ursula stitched and Gudrun went on with her sketch. The sisters were women, Ursula twenty-six and Gudrun twenty-five. But both had the remote, virgin look of modern girls, sisters of Artemis rather than of Hebe. Gudrun was very beautiful, passive, soft-skinned, soft-limbed. She wore a dress of dark-blue silky stuff, with ruches of blue silk lace in the neck and sleeves; and she had cherry-coloured stockings. Her look of confidence and diffidence contrasted with Ursula's sensitive expectancy. The provincial people, ~~were rather~~ intimidated by Gudrun's perfect sang-froid and simple bareness of manner, said of her: "She is a smart woman," ~~they said of her~~. She had just come back from London, where she had spent several years, working at an art-school, as a student, and living a studio life.

"I was preparing myself to make a creditable match," she said, suddenly catching her underlip between her teeth, as if she were hurt by disappointment. ~~"I think I would accept a good offer," she said calmly.~~ ~~Ursula never took her too seriously.~~ Ursula was afraid to be too serious.

"So you have come home, to find the man?" ~~one,~~" she ~~laughed~~ laughed.

"Oh my dear ~~no, you~~," said Gudrun, "I wouldn't go out of my way to look for him. But if there did happen to come along a highly attractive individual ~~decent, eligible person~~ of considerable means, and we caught fire like anything, you know, with each other; – I might immolate myself." – She seemed wistful. – "I'm getting bored," she went on, in pathetic complaint. ~~I'm rather bored, as a matter of fact. Things dont materialise, I find. There~~ "Things don't seem to materialise with me, I find. There's

Page 2 of the Toronto typescript of *Women in Love*. (Courtesy of the Thomas Fisher Rare Book Library, University of Toronto.)

Appendix

> "You wouldn't even accept a good offer?" said Gudrun.
> "Nay," replied Ursula. "But I don't really want to marry, do you?"
> "I think I've rejected several," said Ursula.
> "No very active desire," replied Gudrun. "But would you refuse a
> Really!' A decent man and a decent establishment! Have you really?"
> "A thousand a year, and an awfully nice man. I liked him awfully," said Ursula.
> "Oh yes, inordinately," cried Ursula. "What a horrible thought!" and exclaimed
> "Really! But were n't you fearfully tempted?"
> "In the abstract but not if, the concrete," replied Ursula. "When it comes to the point, one isn't even tempted. Oh, if I were tempted, I'd marry like a shot. – I'm only tempted not to."
> the jaws of both sisters shone with a transcendent amusement.
> "Really good offers!" asked Gudrun.
> "Isn't it an amazing thing," cried Gudrun, "how strong the temptation is, not to marry!"
> "I think so. as far as you ever can tell."
> They both laughed, looking at each other. In their hearts, they were frightened.
> There was a long pause, whilst Ursula stitched and Gudrun went on with
> her sketch. The sisters were women, Ursula twenty-six and Gudrun twenty-
> five. But both had the remote, virgin look of modern girls, sisters of
> Artemis rather than of Hebe. Gudrun was very beautiful, passive, soft-
> skinned, soft-limbed. She wore a dress of dark-blue silky stuff, with
> ruches of blue silk lace in the neck and sleeves; and she had cherry-
> coloured stockings. Her look of confidence and diffidence contrasted
> with Ursula's sensitive expectancy. The provincial people, were rather
> intimidated by Gudrun's perfect sang-froid and simple bareness of
> manner, [said of her:] " She is a smart woman," they said of her. She had just come
> back from London, where she had spent several years, working at an art-
> school, as a student, and living a studio life.
> "I was preparing myself to make a creditable match," she said, suddenly
> "I think I would accept a good offer," she said calmly, catching her underlip between her teeth, as if she were hurt by disappointment.
> Ursula never took her too seriously.
> Ursula was afraid to be too serious.
> "So you have come home, to find)one," she laughed. The man? exclaimed laughed
> "Oh mind you," said Gudrun, " I wouldn't go out of my way to look my dear
> for one. But if there happened to come along a highly attractive individual tho
> of considerable means, and he were terribly enamoured of me – I, I'm we caught fire like anything. You know, with each other – I might
> getting bored immolate myself – "She seemed wistful. "I'm getting bored," she went on,
> rather bored, as a matter of fact. Things don't materialise, I find. There in pathetic complaint. "Things don't seem to materialise with me, I find. There's

Page 2 of the Texas typescript of *Women in Love*. (Courtesy of the Humanities Research Library, University of Texas at Austin.)

Appendix

249

"Badly, I'm sure ~~I should think~~; seeing how self-conscious she is."

"She is self-conscious is she? Then what made her do it? For I assure you it was quite uncalled for, and quite unjustified."

"I suppose ~~the sudden desire overcame~~ it was a sudden impulse her."

"Yes, but ~~why should she want to do such a thing?~~ how do you account for her having such an impulse? I've done her no hurt."

~~Birkin shook his head~~
~~"I couldn't tell you. I suppose she did want to—"~~
"The Amazon suddenly came up in her I suppose," he said.
~~Gerald was thinking how he had said to her, that she had struck the first~~
"I tell you," replied Gerald, "I'd rather it had been the Orinoco."
~~blow, and how she had replied that she would strike the last; and he was on~~
He was thinking how Gudrun had said she would strike the last blow too. But some deep
~~the point of telling Birkin this also. But something made him keep it back.~~
reserve made him keep this back from Birkin.

"And do you resent it?" Birkin asked.

"I dont <u>resent</u> it. I don't care a tinker's curse about it." He was silent a moment, then he added, laughing, "No, I rather like her for it.—She seemed sorry /afterwards." herself

"Did she? You've not seen her since that night?"

Gerald's face clouded.

"No," he said. "We've been – you can imagine how we've been since the accident."

"Has it calming down?" ~~in a state~~ !
~~"I don suppose everybody's terribly upset."~~

"I don't know. It's a shock, of course. But I don't believe mother minds. I really don't believe she takes any notice. And what's so funny, she used to be all for the children – nothing mattered, nothing whatever mattered but the children. And now, she doesn't take any more notice than if it was one of the servants."

"No? ~~Shakespeare has no reason~~ Did it upset <u>you</u> very much?"

"It's a shock. But I don't feel it much now. I don't feel any different. We've all got to die, so why make any bones about it. Death's there, we know it, and we might as well just accept it – whenever or however it comes. It's just death, and there it is. It's nothing new."

Page 249 of the Texas typescript of *Women in Love*. (Courtesy of the Humanities Research Library, University of Texas at Austin.)

159

Appendix

249

" Badly, I should think; seeing how self-conscious she is."

" She is self-conscious is she? Then what made her do it? For I assure you it was quite uncalled for, and quite unjustified."

" I suppose ~~the sudden desire overcame her.~~" *It was a sudden impulse.*

" Yes, but ~~why should she want to do such a thing?~~" *how do you account for her having such an impulse? I'd done her no harm.*

Birkin shook his head.

" ~~I couldn't tell you, I suppose she did want to.~~"

The Amazon suddenly came up in her, I suppose, he said.

~~Gerald was thinking how he had said to her, that she had struck the first blow, and how she had replied that she would strike the last; and he was on the point of telling Birkin this also. But something made him keep it back.~~ *"I tell you," replied Gerald, "I'd rather it had been the Orinoco." He was thinking how Gudrun had said she would strike the last blow too - But some deep reserve made him keep this back from Birkin.*

" And do you resent it?" Birkin asked.

" I dont <u>resent</u> it. I don't care a tinker's curse about it." He was silent a moment, then he added, laughing," No, I rather like her for it. She seemed *hugely* sorry afterwards."

" Did she? You've not seen her since that night?"

Gerald's face clouded.

" No," he said." We've been - you can imagine how we've been since the accident."

" Yes. ~~I suppose everybody's fearfully upset.~~" *Is it calming down?* *in a state!*

" I don't know. It's a shock, of course. But I don't believe mother minds. I really don't believe she takes any notice. And what's so funny, she used to be all for the children - nothing mattered, nothing whatever mattered but the children. And now, she doesn't take any more notice than if it was one of the servants."

" No? ~~She's broken the connection.~~ Did it upset <u>you</u> very much?"

" It's a shock. But I don't feel it much now. I don't feel any different. We've all got to die, so why make any bones about it. Death's there, we know it, and we might as well just accept it - whenever or however it comes. It's just death, and there it is. It's nothing new."

Page 249 of the Toronto typescript of *Women in Love*. (Courtesy of the Thomas Fisher Rare Book Library, University of Toronto.)

Index

Index

Aldington, Mrs. Hilda, 110
Andrewes, Esther, 110

Balzac, Honoré de, 37
Beaumont, C. W., 97, 122
Best, Marshall, 53n
Bibesco, Antoine, 122
Bowers, Fredson, 59n, 60
Branda, Eldon, 130n
"Brangwensaga," 5, 27
Burnet, John: *Early Greek Philosophers*, 145

Carswell, Catherine, 98, 105–6n, 109, 116
Carswell, Donald, 98, 109
Creativity, nature of
   and censorship, 46–52, 127–28
   craft vs. inspiration, 5–7
   discovery, not disguise, 142
   drama vs. didacticism, 143
   Huxley's notion of "daimon," 5
   "living rhythm of whole work," 82
Crown, The, 80–81, 101, 143, 147

Daleski, H. M., 51

Index

David (Old Testament), 44–45
Davis, Herbert, 99–100
Delavenay, Emile, 99n, 100n, 117, 131, 132
Dickerson, Sir John, 57
Draft, definition of, 10–11
Duse, Eleanor, 109

Eliot, T. S., 81

Farmer, David, 125
Flaubert, Gustave, 6
Ford, George, 99, 112, 118
Frank, Waldo, 120

Garnett, Edward, 8, 15, 20
"Goats and Compasses," 101
Gregg, W. W., 60

Heraclitus, 143–44, 147
Heseltine, Philip, 97, 101, 129–30
Hirsch, E. D., 61
Hone, J. M., 121
Huebsch, B. W., 52, 57, 120–21, 124
Huxley, Aldous, 5–6

"Insurrection of Miss Houghton, The," see *Lost Girl, The*

Jennie (*The Rainbow*), 46–47, 75
Joyce, James, 6, 52

Kennerley, Mitchel, 23
Kinkead-Weekes, Mark, 6, 11, 16, 17n, 19n, 21, 24–27, 31, 33
Koteliansky, S. S., 30, 116–17

Lacy, Gerald, 33n, 99n

Index

Lady Chatterley's Lover, 6, 37
Lawrence, Frieda
  as model for Ella, 16
  role in *Women in Love* transcription, 153–54
  and title of *The Rainbow*, 23
Leavis, F. R., 6
Lee, K., 78
Lost Girl, The, 15, 102
Low, Barbara, 110
Lowell, Amy, 30, 103

McLeod, A. W., 8
Methuen publishers
  abandon *The Rainbow*, 40–41n
  and advance on *The Rainbow*, 38
  demand bowdlerizations, 39–40
  refuse "The Wedding Ring," 23
Meynell, Viola, 35, 77–78
Michal (Old Testament), 44
Mistress of Tom Brangwen, 42–44
Moore, Harry T., 3n, 124n
Morrell, Ottoline, 33, 35, 76–77, 97, 109–10, 124;
    as model for Hermione Roddice, 110n

Palmer, Cecil, 97, 120
Pinker, J. B., 28, 32, 35–36, 39–41, 53n, 97, 102–5, 108, 117, 120
Prussian Officer, The, 28

Rainbow, The,
  characters in
    Brangwen, Anna, 44–46, 49–51, 66–67, 75, 84–87
    Brangwen, Lydia, 29, 31, 42, 62–64
    Brangwen, Tom, 29, 31, 42–44, 62–65, 84
    Brangwen, Uncle Tom, 79

Index

Rainbow, The, (*cont.*)
    Brangwen, Ursula, 29, 33–34, 54–56, 70–71, 82–85, 88–89, 92–93
    Brangwen, Will, 46–52, 66–69, 75, 84–87
    Harby, Mr., 69–71
    Inger, Winifred, 24, 31
    Schofield, Anthony, 54
    Schofield, Maggie, 54
    Skrebensky, Anton, 32–35, 55–56, 82–85, 88–89, 92–93
  critical edition, need for, 58–61
  editing, principles of, 41–42
  editorial interference in, 37–41
  final manuscript
    preparation of, 73–81
    revision, examples of, 81–94
  fourth draft of "The Sisters," 28–36
  and Lawrence's fear of censorship, 35–36, 38–41
  proof alterations in
    compulsory changes, 42–48, 52–57
    variants, 37–38
    voluntary changes, 49–52, 61–72
  prosecution and burning of, 39–41, 57
Rainbow, the (image), 71–72
"Rainbow Books and Music, The," 101
Roberts, Warren, 10, 99–101

Savage, Henry, 8
Secker, Martin, 109, 119, 126–30
Seltzer, Thomas, 119, 124–26, 128
Signature, The (magazine), 101
"Sisters I" (first draft of "The Sisters")
  characters in
    Brangwen, Gudrun, 17–18
    Crich, Mrs., 19
    Crich, Gerald, 17–18
    Crich, Winifred, 19

Index

"Sisters I" (first draft of "The Sisters") (*cont.*)
    Ella, 16–17
    Loerke, 17
  Garnett's criticism of, 16
  précis of, 17–19
  and problem of voice, 17
"Sisters II" (second draft of "The Sisters")
  characters in
    Birkin, Rupert, 20–22
    Crich, Gerald, 20–21
    Ella, 20–22
    Templeman, Ben, 20, 22
  generational depth in, 21
  précis of, 21–22
Sons and Lovers, 15, 37, 79
Study of Thomas Hardy, The, 28

Tedlock, E. W., Jr., 124n
Twilight in Italy, 101

Vitoux, Pierre, 118n

"Wedding Ring, The" (third draft of "The Sisters")
  characters in
    Ella, 24–25, 27, 69
    Harby, Mr., 69
    Skrebensky, Charles, 24
  generational depth in, 26–27
  as magnum opus, 23
  rejection as indecent, 23
Women in Love
  first draft
    "Prologue," 99, 110–12
    "The Wedding Chapter," 99, 110–12
  second draft
    "Exeunt" (rejected epilogue), 113–14

Index

Women in Love (cont.)
    written in student notebooks, 103-4
  third (penultimate) draft
    duplicate typescripts of, 104-9, 151-60
    Frieda's role in transcription of, 106-8, 153-54
    and libel threats, 109-10
    read by friends, 105, 110
    rejected by publishers, 105
    titles of, 113
  fourth (final) draft
    bowdlerization of, 126-29
    characters in
      Birkin, Rupert, 111, 128-29, 135, 136-48
      Brangwen, Gudrun, 113-14, 133, 145
      Brangwen, Ursula, 113, 128, 142-48
      Crich, Mrs., 111
      Crich, Gerald, 111, 127, 132-36, 137-42
      Halliday, 126, 130, 146; *see also* Heseltine, Philip
      Pussum, 130; *see also* Heseltine, Philip
      Roddice, Hermione, 109-10
      Leitner, 127
      Loerke, 111, 127
    delay of publication, 116, 124
    editions of, 124-30
    editing, suggestions for, 125-26
    and libel threats, 124, 129-30
    private schemes for publication of, 116, 120-22
    proof changes in
      forced, 126-30
      voluntary, 127-28
    revision in manuscripts of
      discussion of, 131-48
      two phases, 118-23
    transatlantic publication of, 124